Nevertheless

What the Bible Says About Mental Health

CHYINA POWELL

To Su, Ngaio, Gabe and Uncle Brother
For being a city on a hill

Nevertheless he regarded their affliction, when he heard their cry: And he remembered for them his covenant, and repented according to the multitude of his mercies.

~Psalm 106:44-45

Foreword

Who I Am:

I am a young Christian, striving to be better. At times it is an excruciating process because I feel too tired to keep battling the flesh. I want to give up. The war is already won so letting flesh win one battle isn't a big deal, right? I used to think that way and sometimes I still do. But as I have come to know the Father, I now know that the battles do matter. Each and every one. We have to fight the good fight because if we don't, we may wander away from God.

    I am not a deaconess or a pastor or a praise team leader. I have never spoken to thousands or performed on large stages. But you know what? That doesn't mean I am not a follower of Christ. It doesn't mean I am less saved or less holy than those who do. The Bible says that everyone has their own place in the body (1 Corinthians 12:20-30). And we are all indispensable. I am someone who is learning to trust God with what He has me over instead of yearning to do something else. If I get to be the nail on the pinky toe, at least I am a part of His body! I am someone who wants to share God's love and His unyielding faithfulness and commitment.

    That is why I began to blog. My blog, Rise Holy, is geared towards reminding the world that your stumble doesn't matter. You may even fall but that doesn't matter. What matters, what truly matters, is that you rise. And when you rise, that you rise holy! I am a believer and, hopefully, if you aren't already, you will be one at the end of this study.

Why This Book:

Nevertheless is a Bible-based study meant to help offer encouragement to anyone and everyone who has ever felt alone, anxious, depressed, unloved or unheard. This study really grew out of my own desire to remember how loved I am. We live in a sad and fallen world, and that means that we deal with a lot of stress, regret and sometimes the world seems to be on our shoulders.

You might feel disconnected or out of touch, like everyone is on the same page but you. That is just a part of living in the world. I know it, I've experienced it firsthand but we are to be in the world, not of it, which means that we don't have to feel anxious or unloved or burdened anymore. Why? Because we are seen, loved and valuable, even when we don't feel like it.

This 28-session guide will remind you of who God is, who you are in Him, and your rights as His child. It is time to reclaim your identity! Jesus came to give us an abundant life (John 10:10) and that includes all aspects of our life, including mental health. I have found that too many Christians feel ashamed of their mental and emotional health struggles. Luckily, the Father meets us right at the point of our need. He sees what you're going through and He wants to help you through it.

This study can be done either alone or in a Bible Study group. For those who use this book in a group, ask your group members to be vulnerable, to ask their own questions and to talk out other helpful ways we all can see God in our situations and learn to overcome the metal battles surrounding us on a daily basis.

And remember, the goal of this study is to learn. To learn that you aren't alone in your struggles. To learn that God s right beside you and He understands. To learn you are worth so much more than you think. To learn that you can and will overcome once you start to take God at His Word

The Power Of A Word:

"Nevertheless" is a term not a lot of people come across nowadays. It is word that means "in spite of," "notwithstanding," and "however." It is a word used 97 times in the KJV Bible. Nevertheless is a powerful word and more than that, it is a tool. In the following sessions, you shall see the word repeatedly and with luck it will sink into your spirit so that when situations arise you are able to say, "This sucks nevertheless God is good/this is a day He's made/I am victorious!" Or something along those lines.

You will see at the back of the study are some perforated sheets. Feel free to rip them out and post them somewhere easily accessible so that you are reminded of the power of the Lord in your life. This guide is meant to be used so highlight it, write in it, ask questions. I want you to go deeper than you ever have before in regards to this relationship thing.

Week One

I'm Not Good Enough
Nevertheless God Enables Me

DAY 1

The Truth About Comparison

Living in a fallen world, we are taught at an early age to compare ourselves to others, to covet the things we don't have. Commercials and ads that we see every day tell us that we won't be happy until we have Product A, that we are boring and plain unless we buy Product B, that in order to be good looking you need these facial features, these measurements. The world trains us to believe we aren't good enough, trying to convince us that the only way to be truly valuable is to remake ourselves into its image. This is true for both men and women, everyone who lives at one time or another felt that they weren't worthy. Why? Because we internalize what we see and what we hear and all too often that includes negative beliefs and condescending remarks. And once such things take root in your mind, it can be hard to pull them out.

Write down a time you felt you weren't good enough. Was it brought on by something you saw in the media? Has your perspective changed? How?

_____

_____

_____

_____

_____

_____

_____

_____

The world wants us to believe that we are unimportant, that we could never amount to anything. It teaches us to compare ourselves to others and leads us to envy, bitterness, and quite often depression. But this is the way of the world. This is not God's way.

True, Adam's sin led to all mankind being born in sin but in Jesus, our Messiah, we have been redeemed. So, while at one point we were not good enough (in fact, Isaiah 64: 6 says we were unclean), we have now been redeemed. Redemption means that we have returned to God, that our sin has been washed clean, every little stain on our hearts is gone. In our sin, we weren't good enough but once we accept Christ as our Lord and Savior and determine in our hears to have a personal relationship with Him, **He makes us good.**

> We are good enough:
> To touch lives
> To walk in our calling
> To bless others
> To change situations
> In fact, we are good enough to be called the children of God!

> *But when the fulness of the time was come, God sent forth his Son, made of a woman, made under the law,*
> *To redeem them that were under the law, that we might receive the adoption of sons.*
> *And because ye are sons, God hath sent forth the Spirit of his Son into your hearts, crying Abba, Father.*
> *Wherefore thou art no more a servant but a son; and if a son then an heir of God through Christ.*
>
> Galatians 4:4-7

The Bible tells us that not only do we stop being a slave to sin but that now we are His children and His heirs. And guess what? God is a good Father. He provides all that His children could ever need.

> *If ye then being evil, know how to give good gifts unto your children, how much more shall your Father which is in heaven give good things to them that ask him?*
>
> Matthew 7:11

Our Heavenly Father gives us good gifts because He loves us. He makes us to be conquerors here in the Earth. Our Lord strengthens, heals, protects, comforts and so much more. And when there is something that He asks us to do, He enables us to do it.

What does this mean?

If God calls you to preach or teach, He'll give you the boldness to do it.

If He calls you to pray for someone, He'll give you the words to say.

If He says you're to go out and help the needy, He'll provide you with all the tools you need.

You see, God doesn't call the qualified, He qualifies the called so that He may get the glory.

Day 1

For ye see your calling, brethren, how that not many wise men after the flesh, not many might, not many noble, are called:

But God hath chosen the foolish things of the world to confound the wise; and God hath choen the weak things of the world to confound the things which are mighty;

And base things of the world, and things which are despised, hath God chosen, yea, and things which are not, to bring nought things that are:

That no flesh should glory in his presence.

1 Corinthians 1:26-29

What does this passage mean? You don't have to be the smartest, bravest, richest, prettiest, most talented person in the world. You don't have to measure up to the world's standard because we now have a new standard: Jesus. We are called to be like Him and, thanks to redemption, it is possible for us. And when the Lord requires you to do something out of your wheelhouse and forces you out of your comfort zone, He will definitely give you everything you need to accomplish the task He's set before you.

Name a time God called you out of your comfort zone. Did you obey?

_____

_____

_____

_____

_____

_____

If so, how did it change you and your relationship with God? If not, what held you back?

_____

_____

_____

_____

_____

WEEK ONE

What have you learned from that experience?

_____
_____
_____
_____
_____

This week we will be focusing on men and women of God who, through no strength or virtue of their own, were able to do great things. Don't think for a second that great things only mean changing nations or leading armies or healing or raising people from the dead. Sharing your testimony is a great act. Helping those in need with a smile on your face is a great act. We, as believers, tend to think of miracles as only the "big" things. I struggle with this as well because in the world we are taught that :great" equals big and loud and public. Therefore, the work we do for the Kingdom may seem pretty insignificant to us but the Lord doesn't think that way. Why do you think so much of Jesus' ministry focused on love and showing kindness? Because it is important to God! What you're doing matters and God sees your hard work. And when He does ask you to do something bigger, He'll give you everything you need.

Name 3 "little" ways you can add to the kingdom of God.

_____
_____
_____

Remember, you are significant to the Father. You aren't useless. Repeat this to yourself a few times: "I feel unable nevertheless God enables me."

DAY 2

Feeling Inadequate

Yesterday, I gave a brief overview of this week's focus: feelings of inadequacy. Today we will focus on Sarai and Mary Magdelene, one woman from the Old Testament and one from the New.

Read Genesis 18:9-14.

Many of you know this story. Abram and his wife Sarai are old and living in tents. The couple hasn't had any children and yet God promises Abram more descendants than stars in the sky. (Feel free to read the whole story starting at chapter 14.) The Lord promised this and even changed their names to Abraham and Sarah, yet years went by and they still didn't have children. Impatient, Sarah declares it is impossible for her to have kids and tells her husband to sleep with her handmaiden. I can imagine how bitter she was thinking she wasn't a part of the promise God made to her husband. And once Hagar, her maid, had a son, Hagar began holding it over Sarah's head, as though Sarah was the one with the issue. Like she was the problem. And of course, Abraham treated his son Ishmael with love and care and, by extension, Hagar.

But the story doesn't end there. One day, the Lord tells Abraham that his wife (Sarah) will bear a child. Sarah overhears and laughs at the word of God! Why? Because in the natural the idea of having children at her age is ridiculous. But guess what, at ninety years old she gives birth to Isaac.

There was no medical way Sarah could've birthed a healthy baby boy. That was impossible but with God, it was a simple matter. And Isaac became the recipient of the covenant of God, as were all his descendants.

Read Genesis 21:1-7.

Sarah lived to be 127 years old. She was impatient and grievous. She thought herself useless because she couldn't bare her husband an heir (which was *really* important in those days). She felt inadequate and yet God moved through her. What she couldn't do on her own, God did.

WEEK ONE

Name a time where it was obvious that God moved on your behalf.

_____
_____
_____
_____
_____

How did you thank Him? What did His help mean to you then? What does it mean to you now?

_____
_____
_____
_____
_____

Let's move on to Mary Magdelene.

A lot of people know that Mary Magdelene was one of Jesus' followers but who was she? Why did she choose to follow Him? Luke 8:2-3 tells us this:

And certain women, which had been healed of evil spirits, and infirmities, Mary called Magdalene, out of whom went seven devils,

And Joanna the wife of Chuza Herod's steward, and Susanna, and many others, which ministered unto him of their substance.

If a man comes and not only heals your body but casts seven demons out of you, I'd imagine you'd be pretty grateful. And out of gratitude, and most likely a bit of curiosity, Mary Magdalene stayed to hear Christ speak to the people. We also know that after hearing Jesus teach, Mary Magdalene chose to be His disciple and follow Him, providing financial support to the ministry of our Messiah.

I want to draw your attention to a few scriptures:

John 19:25
Mark 15:45-47
Mark 16:1-2

Day 2

The Bible doesn't give us a lot of insight not Mary Magdalene, but these verses let us know that she was truly a dedicated woman. Not everyone who claimed to be a disciple was there while Jesus hung from the cross. But Mary Magdalene was there, standing right with Mary, mother of Christ. Moreover, Mary Magdalene went and tended to the Lord's body, anointing Him while He was in the tomb and it was she that was one of the women to find the stone rolled away on the third day! She was faithful and dedicated even when others had given up hope and she was rewarded by being one of the *first in the entire world* to know Christ had risen (Mark 16:5-6). The Lord had kept His word and truly was who He said He was.

Mary Magdalene was a woman who decided to follow Christ after He healed her. What does this have to do with feeling inadequate? Imagine it, you're already not considered a citizen because you are a woman, you can't teach or do much honorable work outside the home and one day you up and decide to follow a strange man you don't know. Anyone can agree that's a lot to handle but get this, Mary was constantly witnessing the Lord Jesus speak and teach and heal and deliver and yet she couldn't do any of that. All she could do was give money when she could to fund the ministry and be faithful.

Have you ever been in a situation surrounded by people you thought were better than you? How did it make you feel?

_____

_____

_____

_____

_____

Have you ever wanted to truly be a part of something but felt like you would always be an outsider?

_____

_____

_____

_____

_____

_____

_____

Mary Magdalene was a human, just like us so it is safe to presume she had a longing to give more to the Kingdom in some way. She probably felt that the "little" she did was insufficient. She wasn't healing the blind or casting out demons or cutting off ears. But the Lord knew everything she did. And while she didn't do a lot in her eyes or to the standard of man, she did something. God knew her heart. Even after Christ's death, she wanted to show her loyalty and love for the Son which is why she anointed his body with oils. She more than likely spent a great deal of money on the oils and spices too, but that's because she loved Him. The Lord saw her and the love in her heart.

God looks at the heart! So, what if you can't go on an expensive international mission trip? You can give time here and now. Do what you can do for God. He isn't asking us to give Him what we don't have, He isn't a cruel Lord. He knows us and our capabilities. The Father only asks that if we can do something, we do it.

There's a song by Sullivan Pugh that I've always loved. At one point in the song he says, "Now the work I've done seems so small, / Sometimes it seems like, seems like nothing at all. / But when I stand before my God, I want to hear Him say well done. / May the work I've done speak for me."

How grandiose or public your work is doesn't matter. If you're doing all you can with what you have, He'll be pleased.

We focused on impatient and sorrowful Sarai who through no goodness of her own brought forth an entire nation. And then we switched gears and looked at Mary Magdalene who was never recorded as having performed miracles or did some sort of spectacular thing, but she was still able to serve the Son wholeheartedly.

What have you learned from reading the stories of these women? How can you apply it to your life?

_____

_____

_____

_____

_____

_____

DAY 3

We Are Becoming Who We Are Meant To Be

Today our study looks at Gideon, a mighty man of valor. But he didn't start that way. In fact, Gideon was a bit of a coward.

Read Judges 6.

What is your first impression of Gideon?

_____

Read Judges 6:12 again. What does the angel call Gideon?

_____

_____

Gideon wasn't acting much like a valiant man, he was making every excuse to get out of what God asked him to do. But remember this: The Lord knows us and He knows who we are becoming even if we don't. Gideon wasn't a mighty man of valor in verse 12 but God was calling him by what he *would be*. The Father known us inside and out. He sees the potential is us even when we fail to recognize it.

Now read Judges 7.

WEEK ONE

Does Gideon change from chapter 6 to chapter 7? How so?

_____
_____
_____
_____
_____

Gideon does what the Lord asks even though he was afraid, even though they were going up against a powerful army with only a few hundred men. Much like in chapter 6, Gideon was afraid, but the difference is that he doesn't let his fear lead him to disobey God.

If you like, feel free to read chapter 8 to see how Gideon's story ends but I want to focus on chapters 6 and 7.

Gideon tested God multiple times and came up with excuse after excuse. To man, they were pretty valid excuses. Gideon was a nobody and a coward, how could someone like him ever do anything worthwhile or amazing? Besides, he's just him. Nobody special, just a young man living in a place surrounded by idol worshippers. Why would the Lord ever want to use him? He isn't worthy.

That is how man thinks. We doubt ourselves because we've been told that we weren't good enough or we've compared ourselves to others and in our eyes we have fallen short. We aren't important enough or good enough or smart enough to be of any use to God.

Have you ever thought like this?

_____

List a few of your "enoughs" and why you believe(d) them.

_____
_____
_____
_____
_____
_____
_____

Day 3

Let's think about chapter 7. God tells Gideon to get rid of most of his army and he does. Why? So that Gideon and his army will know that they victory came through the Lord, not their own power. Pretend you're Gideon for a moment. You are about to go to war and you have over 20,000 men which might, just maybe, be enough. Now imagine that God tells you to get rid of over 22,000 of them! By man's standard 300 people isn't enough to win a war but for God, it was more than enough.

You read what happened next, how Gideon's army doesn't even have to fight, the enemy fled and killed their own. Why would God go through all this trouble to show Himself to a coward when He could've sent anybody to lead this army? True, Gideon and his army did kill people but couldn't God have chosen someone a bit braver? Someone more important? Simple answer: yes. But here's why He didn't.

For ye see your calling, brethren, how that not many wise men after the flesh, not many mighty, not many noble, are called:
But God hath chosen the foolish things of the world to confound the wise; and
God hath chosen the weak things of the world to confound the things which are mighty;
And base things of the world, and things which are despised, hath God chosen, yea, and things which are not, to bring to nought things that are:
That no flesh should glory in his presence.

1 Corinthians 1:26-29

God purposefully uses those others would think little of, the underdogs, the simple, the unassuming, the weak, the foolish, the despised to do His will so that He can get the glory.

Describe a time where something happened to you and you knew it had to be God.

_____
_____
_____
_____
_____

How did you know?

_____
_____
_____

This is what I want to say to you in this moment.

You aren't too old to be used by God.
You aren't too dumb to be used by God.
You aren't too poor to be used by God.
You aren't too ugly to be used by God.
You aren't too messed up to be used by God.
You aren't too cowardly to be used by God.
You aren't too weak to be used by God.
You aren't too unsophisticated to be used by God.

God can use anyone so thank Him that He chose you! And just like how He gave Gideon everything he needed to fight and be victorious, the Lord will give you everything you need. Gideon didn't start out as a mighty man of valor, he became one. And the same God is working in you. Has He spoken to you about what you're becoming? If so, thank Him for the revelation. If He hasn't yet, ask Him for revelation and thank Him for choosing you and equipping you!

And remember, the God who started a great work in you is more than faithful enough to bring it to completion (Philippians 1:6).

DAY 4

Perfection Isn't Reality

When I think of a king, I think of some pompous man in a crown, wearing a purple robe and lording over others because he was born believing he was better than them. I certainly don't think about shepherds or murderers or sinners. But that is exactly who King David was.

Read 1 Samuel 17:12-29.

David had been out tending the sheep when his father tells him to go bring lunch to his older brothers at the battlefront. He wasn't important enough to fight nor was he old enough, he was just a boy and yet this boy slays the giant Philistine named Goliath in verses 48 through 51.

Have you ever felt like people were looking down on you? Did you feel angry or annoyed? Or did you feel like a failure, like maybe they were right about you?

_____

_____

_____

_____

_____

_____

How old were you?

_____

WEEK ONE

Sometimes people look down on us because we are younger, smaller or different from what they expect us to be. Paul tells Timothy not to let anyone despise him because of his youth but to keep serving God and doing what he knows to do.

Let no man despise thy youth; but be thou an example of the believers, in word, in conversation, in charity, in spirit, in faith, in purity.

1 Timothy 4:12

You are never too young to serve God, never too unimportant. Like we learned in yesterday's study, the Lord uses those no one expects to do mighty works. And every work we do for the kingdom is mighty.

David was the hero no one anticipated. He had been anointed by Samuel as king in 1 Samuel 16:11-13 and at the time, his relationship with King Saul (the current king) was pretty good. But soon Saul started to get jealous of David and spent quite a bit of time and effort trying to kill him. It would take an entire book to talk about David's life but there are some points I want to focus on.

1. David was the youngest son of Jesse yet he was appointed King (1 Samuel 16:11-13).
2. David was a shepherd but managed to slay a giant (1 Samuel 17:48-51).
3. David became a great warrior for the Lord (1 Samuel 18).
4. <u>David wasn't perfect.</u>

How could an imperfect man be called a friend of God? From what we've seen thus far, David was living a righteous life. I mean, because he loved the Lord, instead of killing Saul when he had the opportunity, David spared Saul's life on numerous occasions. Bible studies often focus on the exploits of David but there aren't many that note how he was a peeping tom and a murderer.

Read 2 Samuel 11:2-17.

Yes, you read it right, David got up in the middle of the night and watched a beautiful woman bathing. And when he found out she was married, did he care? Nope. He had his men take her from her home, slept with her and sent her back. Keep in mind that her husband was a faithful warrior, currently fighting on the battlefield, like David should have been. Time passed and Bathsheba told the king she was pregnant, and it obviously couldn't be her husband's child. But instead of coming clean about his actions to Uriah (Bathsheba's husband), David purposefully sends him to the messiest and most violent battlefront so that he can be killed. And King David's plan worked.

What?! But the story doesn't end there. As soon as Bathsheba was finished mourning, David took her and married her. That child died soon after, but their second child was Solomon.

Day 4

And when the wife of Uriah heard that Uriah her husband was dead, she mourned for her husband. And when the mourning was past, David sent and fetched her to his house, and she became his wife, and bare him a son. But the thing that David had done displeased the Lord.

2 Samuel 11:26-27.

David's actions were wrong and the Bible says they displeased the Lord which is why the child died.

Have you ever done something you knew to be wrong?

_____

Did you try to cover it up like David? Or did you decide to be honest and open about your mistakes? Why?

_____
_____
_____
_____
_____

David is called a man after God's own heart (1 Samuel 13:14, Acts 13:22) and yet he made some pretty big mistakes. Here he is breaking quite a few of the Mosaic laws, He killed, committed adultery, and coveted his neighbor's wife. Yet God still loved him.

The Lord loves us even when we make mistakes. He loves us enough to forgive. He doesn't care about how qualified you look to other people or how many mistakes you may have made in the past. It's never too late to ask for forgiveness, to be redeemed. God can still use you even if you make mistakes. Don't doubt His plan for you!

DAY 5

God Can Use You In The Midst Of Your Mess

*L*et's hop straight into the scripture today:

Read Joshua 2.

Rahab was a prostitute living in the city of Jericho. It's not like she used to be a prostitute and stopped, repented and was made new. No, Rahab was a prostitute during the time of this story, when she saved the two spies that came into her house. And when the king sent guards to demand their whereabouts, Rahab didn't give them up. She wasn't an Israelite, but she'd heard of what the God of the Israelites was capable of.

She hadn't seen the Lord work for herself but Rahab knew of what He'd done for His people. She knew the Lord was the one true God and in exchange for saving Joshua's men, (remember that Joshua led the Israelites after Moses' death) she saved her entire family.

Rahab was nowhere close to perfect. She was a harlot and everyone in Jericho, even the king of the city, knew her profession. But she was still able to do something for the kingdom of God. And get this, this is not where Rahab's story ends. Nope. She's mentioned throughout the Word of God.

Matthew 1:1-16 gives us the genealogy of Jesus. As we know, Jesus was a descendent of David. We hear that in Sunday school and in sermons again and again. But did you know that David was the great grandson of Boaz, Ruth's second husband?

And Salmon begat Booz of Rachab; and Booz begat Obed of Ruth; and Obed begat Jesse;

Day 5

And Jesse begat David the king; and David the king begat Solomon of her that had been the wife of Urias;
Matthew 1:5-6

Who does the Bible say is the mother of Boaz?

_____

That's right! Boaz is the son of Rahab the prostitute. That means that Jesus, our savior, was descended from a prostitute.

Are you surprised to hear of Christ's genealogy? Why or why not?

_____

_____

_____

_____

But we hear of Rahab again, as well. Read Hebrews 11:29-32.

Hebrews 11 is often called the "Hall of Faith" because it lists some of the most faithful men and women of the Bible. Rahab is listed in this passage even though her greatest act took place while she was in sin.

Name a time God used you while you were still struggling in sin.

_____

_____

_____

_____

God is so good that He doesn't wait for us to be perfect or have it all together. Sometimes the Lord uses us even when we are in the middle of our mess. The world defined Rahab as a harlot, almost every time her name is mentioned, it is accompanied by the word "harlot." She was a woman of ill-repute, someone people would say didn't deserve God's love, she was someone that people believed He couldn't use. But that wasn't the case. God calls who He wants and He's called you, just as He called everyone we've read about this week.

People may judge you by what you did in the past and try to belittle you but remember that God calls you by who you will become, just as he called Gideon a brave man long before he became one.

God chose you before you knew you were chosen. You aren't a nobody. You're somebody to him.

Write the above sentence in your own words.

_____

_____

Rahab was in the middle of sin. God didn't change her before He used her. He used her just as she was in order to save those men. He used her to bring forth the man we know as the Son of Man. She wasn't in the faith at the time and yet the Father still had a use for her.

God isn't asking you to be perfect before you come to Him. He is only asking that you come. The Lord wants us to be available to Him even while we're in the middle of our mess.

Have you ever felt that you had to be perfect?

_____

What made you feel this way?

_____

_____

I want to leave you with this truth and hopefully, you will soak it in and take it to heart: ***God's love isn't the reward for change, it's the resource so that we can change.***

He loves us regardless of where we are or how we live. He loves us so much that He wants to be close to us. His love isn't earned by status or wealth or intelligence or acts. Once you know the truth of His love for you, you can change. Rahab started her story as a prostitute but ended it as a faithful woman, a great-grandmother of the Christ.

How your story starts isn't how it has to end. Amen.

DAY 6

God's Standard Isn't Man's Standard

I think that oftentimes as believers we see those great Christian leaders on TV working miracles, we hear about all those cool things that are happening in the Spirit and we get discouraged instead of encouraged. While it is great that God is moving in their lives, healing and delivering, giving financial blessings, we begin to wonder if we are truly living Christ-like. We think to ourselves, "If I was living right, if I was a real Christian, wouldn't He have blessed me by now?" We automatically assume that we're doing something wrong because we aren't seeing God move in our lives the same way He moved in someone else's life.

> "Comparison is the thief of joy."
> ~Theodore Roosevelt

I want to point something out to everyone reading this who has ever compared themselves to another, especially to other believers. You are on two separate paths. While your destination may be the same (Heaven), the road we each take to get there is a personal one. Often, we compare and measure ourselves up to others without knowing the full story and wind up feeling inadequate. Today's study will be on someone people tend to judge inaccurately.

Samson's story begins in Judges 13 and ends in Judges 16. He was born to a previously barren woman to be a judge of the Lord's people. In Judges 13:13-25 we hear the story of Samson's birth.

And the angel of the Lord appeared unto the woman, and said unto her, Behold now, thou art barren, and bearest not: but thou shalt conceive, and bear a son.

WEEK ONE

Now therefore beware, I pray thee, and drink not wine nor strong drink, and eat not any unclean thing: For, lo, thou shalt conceive, and bear a son; and no razor shall come on his head: for the child shall be a Nazarite unto God from the womb: and he shall begin to deliver Israel out of the hand of the Philistines

Judges 13:3-5

This passage tells us about Samson's purpose and the one rule he was to live by, that his hair shall never be cut. We tend to believe we know all about Samson. He was a big strong man who could do really cool things but was trapped the moment he fell in love with a Philistine called Delilah. And that he lost his power due to Delilah's deceit.

When you imagine Samson, how do you see his appearance?

_____

_____

Why do you think Samson looked this way?

_____

_____

I invite you to read all of Samson's account in the Scriptures. There is nowhere that describes him as the muscular, scary-looking man you may see in movie adaptations. In fact, it seems that the only time Samson could do marvelous acts was when the Spirit of the Lord came upon him.

Read Judges 15:11-15.

We misjudge Samson and believe that he did such cool feats because of his physical strength but that is where we'd be wrong. Samson by himself wasn't good enough by any means. He needed the power of the Lord to judge the people, which he did for twenty years before Delilah even met him. How many middle-aged men do you know that could carry the doors of a city on his shoulders to the top of a hill (Judges 16:1-3)?

What I want to get you to understand is that you can't assume that someone has made more progress than you, that they're better off than you, that you aren't doing good enough. We have this idea of Samson was because of what he was able to do but he was only able to do such things because of the Spirit of the Lord.

Day 6

How has God used you? Was it because of your power? Or was it the Holy Spirit working in you?

_____
_____
_____
_____
_____
_____
_____
_____

Guess what? That Spirit that came upon Samson now lives in you. Stop saying or thinking you aren't good enough. Why? Because the Lord says you are. You are good enough to house the living God and I'd argue that's pretty good.

DAY 7

Let's Make It A Reality!

To end this week off, I want to go back to where we started. I'm not good enough Nevertheless God can us me. Below there are some blanks that I want you to fill out. It may seem odd but affirmations do change our perspective. The Bible says that "as a man thinketh in his heart, so is he" (Proverbs 23:7). By repeatedly reminding yourself of who God says you are, you can change how you view yourself. I challenge you to repeat these statements once a day for the duration of this study ad see how your view of yourself (and others) shifts.

Fill in the blanks below.

I get impatient Nevertheless _____

I'm not the wealthiest or the smartest or the most talented Nevertheless _____

I'm afraid sometimes Nevertheless _____

People have always looked down on me Nevertheless _____

I make mistakes Nevertheless _____

I feel like God can't use me Nevertheless _____

I compare myself to others Nevertheless _____

God enables those He calls. We may fall short on our own, actually we always fall short on our own, but thank God for His mercy and grace. He doesn't give up on us and He lets us know that in Him we can do anything.

Day 7

I can do all things through Christ which strengtheneth me.
Philippians 4:13

You don't have to be "perfect" to be used by God. The Lord can use you even in the middle of your mess. Use the space below and write a prayer asking God to use you. Be available to Him and watch what He'll do through you.

_____

_____

_____

_____

_____

_____

_____

Also I heard the voice of the Lord, saying, Whom shall I send, and who will go for us? Then said I, Here am I; send me.
Isaiah 6:8

Will you make yourself available to God?

Week Two

I Feel Alone Nevertheless God Never Leaves Me Behind

DAY 1

Why Do We Feel Lonely?

Draw a tally in the margin if you've ever felt lonely. Draw another if you've ever felt lonely even though you were with other people, maybe even surrounded by them. Draw another if you have felt alone. One more if you ever thought that you would be better off alone. Another if you felt no one really cared about you.

By now, most of us would have a few marks on this page. We all have felt lonely at one time or another, we've all longed to feel truly understood and appreciated. This week we are going to tackle the feeling of loneliness in our lives. I'm going to need you to be open, honest and vulnerable this week.

Write down a time you felt alone.

_____

_____

_____

_____

_____

_____

_____

WEEK TWO

Detail an instance you felt unloved or uncared for.

_____

_____

_____

_____

How did these moments in your life impact you?

_____

_____

_____

Do these wounds still hurt?

_____

Loneliness is a very painful emotion that can leave us a wreck if we let it. And sometimes, those who try to help us say that we should "just get over it" or that "it's not that serious," but when you are the one feeling isolated you don't know how to get over it and pretending you're okay only makes things worse. As we delve into the stories this week, we will look at what God says about loneliness and the other emotions loneliness creates such as doubt, anxiety, low self-esteem, depression and fear. But the one truth that I want you to ingest and keep in your heart this week is this: *God never abandons us, even when we feel like He has.*

Be strong and of a good courage, fear not, nor be afraid of them: for the Lord thy God, he it is that doth go with thee; he will not fail thee, nor forsake thee.

Deuteronomy 31:6

What does it say to do in this verse?

That's right. We are told to be of good courage and to not be afraid of our enemies.

Fill in the Blank: He will not _____ thee, nor _____ thee.

The word "strong" here in the Hebrew [2388] means to be strong, to be constant, to maintain, to withstand to become mighty, to encourage yourself. The Father isn't telling us to go slay armies

Day 1

or climb mountains. He is saying that we need to encourage ourselves when we feel lost and alone, and to keep going regardless of how you feel.

The enemy wants you to stop. He doesn't want us, as God's chosen, to move in our calling and one of the ways he hinders us is to make us feel bad and get us caught up in our emotions so that we can't walk in our purpose and bring God glory through victorious living.

Have you ever let your emotions hinder your progress?

_____

How did you move on?

_____

_____

We will go over how to combat these emotions so that the next time you are in a slump, in despair due to your loneliness, you will be able to do what Deuteronomy 31:6 says and be of good courage.

Rewrite Deuteronomy 31:6 in your own words.

_____

_____

What does that mean to you?

_____

DAY 2

Misunderstandings

We feel lonely for a variety of reasons and sometimes for multiple reasons at the same time. One of these reasons is because we feel misunderstood by our peers, our families, our colleagues, our brothers and sisters in Christ, and at times even our closest friends. Feeling as though no one truly sees you for who you are or values your authentic self is tough. It's painful and gut-wrenching. And it can lead to self-isolation, which is withdrawal from relationships. I know, I've done it. Let's unpack this step by step.

List five situations in which you felt misunderstood. Beside them list the reasons you felt others didn't understand.

_____
_____
_____
_____
_____

Most of us can think of more than five cases but sometimes dredging up past pain hurts, it's like slowly peeling a bandage from your arm. But, you can't move on until that bandage is off so it's okay to be vulnerable in this study. Take a few minutes and ask God to give you comfort and peace as you delve into the hurts of your past.

What do you think causes misunderstandings?

_____
_____

Day 2

Assumptions, lack of communication and miscommunication are the main causes of misunderstandings. Especially today, in a world of texts, emails and social media comments, what we mean can often be misunderstood and end up hurting someone or causing negative feelings to sprout up between even the closest of friendships.

Have you ever misunderstood a situation?

_____

How did you discover your misunderstanding?

_____

_____

Were you able to correct the mistake?

_____

How could you learn from your experience?

_____

_____

_____

_____

It's hard to handle it when you feel misunderstood by your friends but Solomon lets us know that we can be strengthened in these times.

A friend loveth at all times, and a brother is born for adversity.
Proverbs 17:17

Misunderstandings can cause rifts between us and our loved ones and sometimes these rifts feel like canyons we can't cross and that is where loneliness comes in. Everyone wants to matter to those who matter to them and typically, misunderstandings trick us into believing we don't matter to those around us and such feelings cause us to isolate ourselves even further. Let's take a look at Hannah.

Read 1 Samuel 1:1-10.

Hannah was the wife of a man named Elkanah and Hannah was his beloved wife. He had another wife named Peninnah who had bore him children but Elkanah loved Hannah more. And yet the Bible says that Hannah's very soul was bitter.

Why do you think that is?

_____

_____

In Biblical times, a woman's worth had a lot to do with the children she bore. Imagine being told all your life that you had one and only one thing that makes you important and not being able to do it. That had to hurt and yet her husband was there trying to console Hannah. Still, she must've felt as though he didn't get it. He was a man first of all, plus he had children. Even though Hannah obviously wasn't alone, she still felt lonely because no one around her could truly comprehend her sadness and her husband's other wife constantly mocked her for being barren.

> *One good thing about Hannah is that while she isolated herself from other people, she did not isolate herself from God. When you need help, always remember that the Lord is right there and He is on your side.*

What led to Hannah's bitterness and sense of being misunderstood?

_____

_____

It was an assumption. Name an assumption you've made in the past. What did it lead to?

_____

_____

_____

Day 2

Hannah's emotions caused her to self-isolate. She stopped eating, drew away from her husband and went up to the temple where she bore her soul to the Lord. Because of her hurt, she cut herself off from others instead of drawing near to them and being comforted by their compassion.

Have you ever self-isolated? Did it help? Why do you think that is?

_____

_____

_____

We've taken a look into how misunderstandings lead to loneliness, but the real question is how to combat these feelings. Firstly, name three things you tend to do when you get lonely or feel misunderstood. Next to them, write how these 3 habits may hinder more than they help.

_____

_____

_____

To appoint unto them that mourn in Zion, to give unto them beauty for ashes, the oil of joy for mourning, the garment of praise for the spirit of heaviness; that they might be called trees of righteousness, the planting of the Lord, that he might be glorified.

Isaiah 61:3

Christ came to comfort those who mourn, heal the brokenhearted, to relieve the heaviness of our hearts. Sounds pretty good, right? Misunderstandings lead to heavy hearts and we, as believers, can take steps to relieve that heaviness because we have the power and ability given to us by the Spirit of God within us.

I've always been the kind of person who prefers step-by-step solutions to problems and issues. Just giving me a generic "Get over it," upsets me and leaves me stressed because I don't know how to move forward. That is why I want to offer some helpful hints and encouraging scriptures that can help you so the next time you feel misunderstood, you don't fall into the same bad patterns.

Hint 1: Don't allow misunderstandings to linger.

The Bible says not to let the sun go down on your wrath (Ephesians 4:26). Similarly, you can't allow a misunderstanding to cause a rift by choosing not to repair the damage quickly. If you feel like you misunderstood someone, ask for clarification. If you feel like something you say or do may be misconstrued, make sure to clear up any confusion right away. (I get it, most of the time you won't want to, but that's where growth comes in.) But let's be honest, the longer it takes to repair a relationship, the less likely it is that things will return to the way they were.

Hint 2: Don't listen to sad music that perpetuates negative feelings.

Why do we like listening to sad music when we're feeling down? It is something I don't understand but something everyone seems to do. Perhaps it goes back to that old saying, "Misery loves company." When we're down, we want to feel like there are others who understand what we're going through.

Wanting to be understood is perfectly natural but listening to sad music is not the way to go about it. Doing so only causes you to dwell on the negative that is happening in your life and if we aren't careful, it can lead us to doubting those closest to us.

Has this ever happened to you?

_____

Write three song titles that you'll make the conscious decision to listen to instead?

_____

_____

_____

Hint 3: Read a scripture or two.

We have to encourage ourselves and one way to do this is to read a passage of scripture or recite a verse that tends to encourage you or offers you peace.

Here are some of my favorites:

1. Isaiah 12
2. Joshua 1:1-9
3. Nehemiah 8:10

Write three verses or passages that offer you peace.

1. _____
2. _____
3. _____

Day 2

Hint 4: Don't self-isolate!

When you begin to feel lonely or upset, your first instinct is to be by yourself. Going off to cool down or think is okay but don't pull yourself away from others completely. Ask a close friend to help you with this. Ask them to be your accountability partner and whenever you feel like you want to talk something out first go to God and then go to them. A helpful strategy is to have a code word, a word that you can text or say and they immediately know that you need to have a serious conversation with them as soon as possible.

Write two of your own hints below.

_____

_____

Remember: I may feel misunderstood but Nevertheless, I am not alone.

DAY 3

Feeling Misunderstood By God

Yesterday, we dissected a bit about misunderstandings and feeling misunderstood. I asked you to be vulnerable enough to look back at times you were misunderstood or perceived yourself to be misunderstood and how that resulted in a sense of loneliness. Today, we are going to go even deeper into misunderstandings because this week I sincerely want you to have a clear sense of where loneliness stems from and how to combat it in your life. Yesterday, I mentioned that one form of misunderstanding is feeling as though no one truly knows you or that if they got to know you, they wouldn't like the real you.

Have you ever felt this way?

Feelings like these cause us to either hide our true selves and pretend to be someone we are not or they cause us to isolate ourselves. Sometimes, it's a combination of the two. **Firstly, I want you to know that feeling sad or lonely sometimes doesn't make you less of a believer, it doesn't mean you aren't Christian enough.** The Bible tells us that we will have tests and trials, these emotions just happen to be one of them for you. Luckily, we know one more thing about the trials we face:

> *And we know that all things work together for good to them that love God, to them who are the called according to his purpose.*
>
> Romans 8:28

Though this seems rough right now, we are more than conquerors because of His indwelling Spirit and it *WILL* work out for our good!

I would like to share a personal testimony with you today. Growing up, I always felt like an outcast. I preferred books to sports, quiet to large groups. I liked food and ate a lot of it. This led to a lot of teasing, most of which came from my own family, and so when it was time for me to go to school I realized something: if not even my own family liked the way I was, these strangers definitely wouldn't. I became a chameleon, changing colors to fit whatever group I was around. No one ever truly knew me and I was never really close with anyone. People couldn't really hate me or like me because my mask stayed firmly in place. In fact, I got so good at wearing a mask, I lost sight of who I really was.

Did I enjoy this activity or did I do it because it was expected of me? Did I like this food or was it just popular? Even when I was alone (which I preferred) I was no longer sure of who I was and that bothered me. I had acquaintances and colleagues and relatives, not friends and family. I felt lost and I turned inward more and more, but not to reflect, to isolate. And it took years and the love of some really amazing people to help me out of myself and a truly magnificent God to keep me during those dark times. I spent years living in a cocoon of my own making because I assumed no one could love me for me. When I emerged I realized two things:

- I shouldn't focus on those who don't accept me.
- God will always love me.

Have you ever felt like you were wearing a mask?
Do you wear it in public? In private? Both?

_____

_____

What made you decide to put on your mask?

_____

_____

_____

_____

_____

_____

_____

Masks and facades are so dangerous because once we put them on, we grow comfortable and don't want to take them off. We may think "it's better this way" or "this is the only way." And we may even feel as though God would have wanted us this way.

Have you ever felt like you were a mistake or that God didn't understand and/or like you? Be vulnerable and recount the experience below.

_____

_____

_____

_____

_____

> *Nevertheless the foundation of God standeth sure, having this seal, The Lord knoweth them that are his. And, let every one that nameth the name of Christ depart from iniquity.*
>
> 2 Timothy 2:19

Fill in the Blank: The Lord _____ them that are _____.

God knows you. Take a look at the following verses.

> *I am the good shepherd, and know my sheep, and am known of mine. As the Father knoweth me, even so know I the Father: and I lay down my life for the sheep.*
>
> John 10:14-15

> *Then the word of the Lord came unto me, saying, Before I formed thee in the belly I knew thee; and before thou camest forth out of the womb I sanctified thee, and I ordained thee a prophet unto the nations.*
>
> Jeremiah 1:4-5

The Lord knew you before you were even born. He knew every mistake you would make, ever joke you'd laugh at, every tear you'd cry. He knew you and still chose to send His Son to die for you. Why would He do that? Because He loves you. Yes, you! Just as you are, flaws and all.

He understands everything you're going through and He ahs everything you need to get through those situations. Don't feel like you have no one to turn to.

Have you ever felt like you couldn't go to God about something?

_____

Why do you think this is?

Did you feel condemned or ashamed or unworthy? Be introspective and talk your emotions out.

Read the following scriptures.

- John 3:16
- Galatians 2:20
- 1 John 4:12
- Jeremiah 31:3

God's love is unwavering and unfailing. He loved you before you loved yourself. You don't need to put on a mask for God. You aren't a mistake and you weren't an afterthought. The Creator of All Things loves you for you. He understands you because He knows your very soul. Your thoughts aren't hidden from Him. How do we know this?

Read Psalm 139.

God knows everything about us, even the smallest little thought. To unbelievers, that may seem creepy or sketchy but to those in the faith, it should give us comfort. We don't have to perform for God! We don't have to pretend to be someone we're not or work for His love or grab hold and shake Him until He understands us. He knows the authentic us and loves us for who we are and according to Romans 8:38, nothing can separate us from the love of God.

How does knowing God loves the real you make you feel?

Dear reader, I ask that you stop performing. You don't have to be someone you aren't or get the worlds approval. God loves you for who you really are. He knows you and He understands. It's not always easy to remember but that is why I've provided the perforated sheets in the back of this study. Take one out and post it so you can remind yourself that the Lord sees you, He loves you and He understands you.

DAY 4

When You're Friends Don't Get It

Now that we've tackled misunderstandings that often lead to feeling lonely, I want to shift gears a bit. These next couple of days will focus on abandonment. The dictionary definition of abandonment is to forsake utterly, to desert, to withdraw from. That's pretty heavy. As people living in a fallen world, we see cases of abandonment more often than we should. On the news we see children abandoned by parents, commercials with animals abused and left to die, we hear stories of elderly men and women left by their children when they have no means to take care of themselves. It's a sad and painful truth of our society. And it is in direct correlation with feeling lonesome or isolated.

Have you ever felt abandoned by someone you cared about? What were the circumstances?

_____
_____
_____
_____

How did you handle it? How do you feel looking back on that time?

_____
_____
_____
_____

Our main focus will be dealing with abandonment at the hands of friends and loved ones. Sadly, it doesn't take a lot to feel forgotten. Maybe someone in your family forgot your birthday or a friend doesn't seem to remember any of your favorite things. You begin to wonder if you really matter to that person. The truth is, you can feel abandoned even with people around you. Abandonment doesn't only mean being left behind in the physical sense. It also includes feeling disconnected and deserted, which is emotional. And guess what? Not every case of abandonment is "big." Most people hear the word and get a picture in their minds with a mom dropping her baby off at a hospital in the middle of the night during a downpour, and she's soaked because she couldn't think about the weather. But that isn't always the case.

What do you think of when you hear the term "to abandon?"

_____

_____

I think that one of the most prominent Biblical cases of abandonment can be found in the book of Job. Job loved the Lord and was devoted to being obedient to the Father. His obedience caused him to be blessed. He was living a great life. Most of us know the story of how God allowed the devil to try Job to prove that Job's love for God was true and not based on the blessings the Lord had bestowed on him. You might think we're going to talk about the relationship between Job and God but today we will look at the people closest to Job, his wife and his friends.

Read Job 2:1-10.

Right before this passage of scripture, all of Job's children were killed. Now we see Job's health taken away from him, and to top it all off, his wife is accusing God and instead of comforting her husband, she's making him feel worse.

How would you feel in this situation? How would you react?

_____

_____

_____

Day 4

Have you ever needed to be consoled and those around you ended up making you feel worse? Write down the circumstances below and what you wish they would have done instead.

_____
_____
_____
_____
_____

Nobody wants to hear someone tell them they'd be better off dead, especially not a family member. But that is exactly what Job's wife told her husband. The Contemporary English Version reads like this: "his wife asked. 'Why do you still trust God? Why don't you curse him and die?' (Job 2:9)" Instead of being kind and empathetic (they were her kids too), she says that he may as well give up. Her words and meaning are perfectly clear. There is no way to misunderstand or misinterpret this. I will not claim that she is a bad wife but it is clear that she is not as dedicated to the Lord as her husband is or else she would've suggested praying or fasting or the use other spiritual weapons, not accept defeat. Can you imagine how alone Job must have felt in this moment? His children, his wealth, his health and even his wife had left him (his wife in an emotional sense). This man had a lot on his plate, but Job refused to sin with his lips by cursing God.

How do you think you would feel in this situation?

_____
_____
_____

Now, let's talk about Job's friends. Job has three good friends: Eliphaz, Bildad and Zophar. When they first learn of Job's suffering, they mourn with him for seven days (Job 2:11-13) but after hearing Job talk about his pain, all three determine that Job's despair is his own fault. Let's look at what each friend has to say and how Job responds.

Read Job 4:1-9.

According to Eliphaz, why is Job being troubled?

_____
_____

Eliphaz says in verse 21 that the wicked should expect destruction because of their wrongdoing. Isn't it crazy how Eliphaz notes all the good Job has done for others in verses 3 and 4 and how he mourned with him in chapter 2 only to say that Job must deserve this and that he should expect more? What's worse is that in chapter 5, Eliphaz begins to look down on his friend saying what he would do in this situation and how Job needs to hurry up and follow his advice before anything worse happens. Eliphaz was so busy talking and quoting platitudes that his words couldn't be further from the heart-to-heart conversation one should expect from a friend.

Do you believe that Eliphaz had good intentions?

_____

_____

Have you had loved ones come into a situation and try to offer solutions without really listening to you? Did you feel better or worse afterwards?

_____

_____

_____

_____

Such interactions can leave us feeling emotionally destitute and drained. Eliphaz came with good intentions, we see that in how he mourned with Job, but Eliphaz ends up doing more harm than good. The scriptures never say that bad things only happen to bad people and yet that is his belief.

How would you feel if someone told you in the middle of a terrible situation, "You must have deserved it?"

_____

_____

_____

Let's look at Job's friend Bildad. Read Job 8:1-7.

Not only does Bildad blame Job's unrighteousness for his issues, he claims Job's a hypocrite for claiming he's done nothing wrong! In verse 2, Bildad clearly says that Job is full of hot air! That's definitely not something I'd like to hear in the midst of my despair. There are many people who believe in Bildad's approach of "tough love" but realize this my friends, Bildad had forgotten some

Day 4

very important characteristics of our Lord: He is merciful and gracious and ruler of all. Bildad implies that the Lord is sleeping, claiming that if Job were pure and righteous the Lord would wake and help him. But the Lord doesn't sleep! Our Father knew the very ins and outs of Job's situation, even if no one else did.

Behold, he that keepeth Israel shall neither slumber nor sleep.
Psalm 121:4

Has someone close to you ever accused you of lying when you weren't?
Did you try to convince them you were being honest? How?

___

Has tough love ever helped you? Has it harmed you? Think of a person who showed you tough love, is there something you wish you could say to them? Write it below.

___

At this point, you might be thinking that Job needs better friends, and I was right there with you when I first read these stories. But before we dive into that, let's look at Zophar, the last of Job's companions that we'll look at today.

Read Job 11:1-6.

Out of the three, Zophar seems the harshest to me. Yes, Eliphaz was judgmental but he had good intentions. True, Bildad was brutal but he truly believed Job could get out of his plight by going to God in earnest. Zophar is sarcastic and snarky. Sarcasm is hard to deal with when you're hurting. Zophar says that Job is lying outright and that he deserves an even harsher punishment for living such a wicked life. (Mind you, he has been Job's friend for years, if that was the case shouldn't he have been trying to lead Job down the right path?) If you read the rest of the book of Job you will see how his friends try to convince an innocent man of guilt and how Job responds. I want to focus on one of Job's answers because I believe a lot of us would respond in a similar way if we were falsely accused by those we thought had our backs through thick and thin.

Read Job 12:1-6.

Job lashes out at his friends because he is hurt not only by his situation but by them as well. They have blamed him for everything and instead of showing compassion, they use Job's bad situation to make themselves look better by comparison.
Have you ever lashed out because you were hurt or angry? What did you do?

_____

_____

_____

_____

Job uses sarcasm, claiming that his friends are so wise that the moment they die all the world's wisdom will be lost. He was in pain and no one around truly listened to him, instead they looked down on him.
Have you ever been put down by someone close to you? How did you respond?

_____

_____

_____

Day 4

Read the following and highlight any words or phrases that stick out to you.

Job 13:1-8 King James Version (KJV)
Lo, mine eye hath seen all this, mine ear hath heard and understood it.
What ye know, the same do I know also: I am not inferior unto you.
Surely I would speak to the Almighty, and I desire to reason with God.
But ye are forgers of lies, ye are all physicians of no value.
O that ye would altogether hold your peace! and it should be your wisdom.
Hear now my reasoning, and hearken to the pleadings of my lips.
Will ye speak wickedly for God? and talk deceitfully for him?
Will ye accept his person? will ye contend for God?

Why do those words or phrases stick out to you?

_____
_____
_____
_____
_____

Job understands what his friends are saying and he knows that they are just like him, men. All this time, his friends have been speaking for God and Job recognizes that they are speaking out of worldly wisdom, not godly wisdom. So, he asks them to be quiet. Job says that even though he doesn't deserve the treatment he is getting, he will trust God no matter what.

Though he slay me, yet will I trust in him: but I will maintain mine own ways before him.
He also shall be my salvation: for an hypocrite shall not come before him.

Job 13:15-16

Don't give up!

Job's friends continue to accuse him and no matter what Job says, they don't believe that he doesn't deserve the terrible things he is experiencing. They hear him but they aren't listening.
Have you ever felt like no one was listening to what you had to say?

_____

How did you react?

_____
_____
_____
_____

This is a lonely place to be, to be surrounded by those you love and feel like they don't care. And through it all, Job didn't give up on God. He wanted to give up, he even asked the Lord for death (6:9), but he never denies God or curses him like his wife advised. Job was correct in saying that people are people. Humans can't speak for God, claiming to know exactly why He moves the way He does. Isaiah 55:8-9 states,

> *For my thoughts are not your thoughts, neither are your ways my ways, saith the Lord.*
> *For as the heavens are higher than the earth, so are my ways higher than your ways, and my thoughts than your thoughts.*

_____
_____
_____

We can't begin to know what God is thinking or why He does something. Job's friends were basing their arguments against him on worldly knowledge. Even those with the best intentions may end up hurting you and causing you to feel like there's no one in your corner but that doesn't mean they're doing it intentionally. Nor does it mean you should give up. Not on yourself and not on God.

Rewrite Job 13:15 in your own words.

_____
_____
_____

It can be a hard pill to swallow when we feel as though our loved ones don't love us back, but you shouldn't give up or give in. Job knew that God had a purpose for what He was doing even if the process was painful, even if he felt abandoned by his closest friends. It wasn't the end for Job nor is it the end for you. You can make it, you can get through this. Don't listen to those

Day 4

naysayers and doubters. Do what Job did and tell them to hold their peace. Job was emotionally alone. His friends and his wife had left him to despair yet nevertheless, Job trusted in the Father.

Are you struggling to trust God in a situation? Write down the situation and a few ways you can be more trusting.

DAY 5

When It Feels Like God Isn't There

Yesterday's lesson dealt with Job feeling unheard and emotionally alone because of his loved ones. Hopefully, you took the time to assess your own life and those times you may have felt alone or abandoned emotionally or even physically. Today, let's take time to consider feeling abandoned by God. Before we begin this study, I have a few questions to ask you.

Have you ever thought that God doesn't hear you or care about you?

_____

How did that make you feel?

_____

_____

Did you try to get back at God because you felt this way?

_____

_____

_____

_____

Day 5

Did you have a hard time trusting God afterward?

Be strong and of a good courage, fear not, nor be afraid of them: for the Lord thy God, he it is that doth go with thee; he will not fail thee, nor forsake thee.

Deuteronomy 31:6

This is a familiar verse and God reiterates this promise through both the Old and New Testaments. Find two reiterations of this Scripture. One from the Old Testament and one from the New. And don't worry, you can search them on the internet!

1. Old-
2. New-

God promises us that He won't abandon us. It is in His Word, so it must be true. And since we know the Lord always keeps his word (even when we don't), He'll stick to this promise. Our brains know it but there are times when our hearts don't get the message. Or maybe it's the reverse, we truly know God will never leave us lonely, but in our situation it feels as though He has done just that and it is hard to see past our situation in these times and find our God who is standing right next to us.

Have you ever felt this way? Explain the situation below.

_____
_____
_____
_____

Job had a lot on his plate. He just lost his family, his health, everything he'd worked his whole life to acquire from his home to his wealth. That couldn't have been easy. And when he needed comfort, his friends just criticized and abused him. As we go deeper into today's study, I want you to think on how Job must've felt and how you would've felt in that moment. Job knew that nothing he had done had brought on this torment. He was so devout, he even offered sacrifices on others' behalf (Job 1:5). But he still went through this awful trial, not because of something he'd done but so God could get the glory once Job went through and came out victorious. Let me make this clear, not every trial or tribulation is brought on by a sin you committed. Let's look at another example.

Read John 9:1-5.

What do the disciples believe was the cause of this man's blindness?

_____

What did Jesus tell them was the true cause?

_____

Yes, sometimes we do things that require us to be chastised by God because he is just, but there are other times when our tests and trials come to make us strong and bring glory to the Lord, our Father.

Name a time when you felt tested by the Lord.

_____
_____
_____
_____
_____
_____

How did it end?

_____
_____
_____
_____
_____
_____
_____

Day 5

Now look back and write down how you felt while you were going through it.

_____
_____
_____
_____
_____

Did you ever just want God to wave His hand and make you a perfect Christian because the trial was too hard or too long or too tiring?

_____
_____

Tests are hard, that's why they are called tests. We can study as much as we want but sometimes, we still feel unprepared. In the world, you review notes and a textbook, in Christ we can look to the Bible for instruction. The Bible is full of principles we should live by and for every problem the world has, God provides a solution in His Word. However, many times, we can't recall the solution or apply it in the right way because we either didn't realize that our test was open book or because we can't focus enough to look past the issue in order to see the answer. I am not trying to make you feel condemned, but I want to be honest with you so that you can learn to be honest with yourself and God. I want to make sure that you know you aren't alone. *There have been others in similar situations, people who have felt what you may be feeling even now.*

Job had done nothing to cause his plight and when he sought comfort, found none but still he recognized that the Lord had a reason. At first, Job loathes the attention, thinking that he'd rather be ignored by God then have all this come upon him (Job 7:16-21), but as we saw yesterday, Job decides to trust in the Lord and the plan He has even though it seemed to be doing Job more harm than good.

Rewrite Job 13:15 below.

_____
_____

Have you ever been in a situation where someone did something that was displeasing at first and later turned out to be for your benefit?

WEEK TWO

What happened?

_____

_____

_____

How did you feel after it was all said and done?

_____

Things don't always feel good to us even when they are good for us. Whether it's being disciplined by our parents, working out at the gym or eating that super healthy food you cannot stand, but all of these things work out for our benefit. Job didn't know what would happen but this is what's important: **You don't have to understand God's every move to trust Him.**

Job was in the midst of despair and he told God as much. In fact, Job says

> *He hath put my brethren far from me, and mine acquaintance are verily estranged from me. My kinsfolk have failed, and my familiar friends have forgotten me. They that dwell in mine house, and my maids, count me for a stranger: I am an alien in their sight.*
>
> Job 19:13-15

Never forget: You are seen and you are heard.

Ouch. When you're a stranger in your own home you undoubtedly feel lonely and unheard, not only by your natural family but sometimes by your spiritual Father. Earlier I asked you to record a time you felt abandoned by God. In the space below write Job 19:22 in your own words.

Job knew that God was there and yet felt utterly alone, even hated by the Creator because of his awful circumstance. But we know that the Lord didn't hate Job. In fact, read what the Bible says in Job 1:5.

The Lord was proud to have such a faithful servant. And because He knows all things, the Father knew that no matter what Satan did to Job, it wouldn't cause him to curse the Lord. Did Job get angry at God? Yes. Did he get sad? Yes. His anger and sarcasm and depression were all a part of his grieving process. But no matter how upset or confused Job became through his ordeal, he never turned away from God. What does this have to do with loneliness? While Job had others around him and knew that the Lord had His eyes on him, he felt unheard and uncomforted, which leads to loneliness and bitterness no matter how many people may be around. We know that Job felt unheard because he repeatedly asks for answers and yet those answers don't come until Job feels like he is past the point of breaking. When Job asks for answers, he doesn't get them until God decides it is time in chapter 38.

Read Job 30:20-21.

Have you ever poured your heart out to someone and it felt like they weren't listening? What happened? How did you feel?

___

Even though someone else may be near, most of us will agree that when no one is listening we begin to feel lonely. We wonder why they aren't listening and begin to make up reasons such as: They don't care, I'm being immature, I'm not important enough to listen to. When we don't get the response we're anticipating we feel disappointed and start to believe that we are, in some way, lacking.

Note a time where you felt let down by someone you loved.

___

How was your situation similar to Job's?

_____

_____

_____

_____

How did that event make you feel about yourself?

_____

_____

When these feelings of resentment and low self-esteem begin to rise we start to feel isolated and while we may read scriptures such as Hebrews 13:5, yet they bring us little comfort in the moment. Why? Because we forget to go to God and be open with our emotions.

> *Let your conversation be without covetousness; and be content with such things as ye have: for he hath said, I will never leave thee, nor forsake thee.*
>
> Hebrews 13:5

Don't you think that God knew what Job was feeling? He knew how you were feeling in your situation too. He knew that you were hurting and He was right there by your side but you couldn't see Him because your eyes were trained on your problem. Have you ever stared at something for so long that everything around it begins to blur? It's a bit like that. By being overly concerned with the devastation happening around you, you begin to remove God from the picture. It's time to let God back in.

Take five minutes today and be open and honest with God. Talk about a time you felt alone or abandoned and don't sugarcoat it. He knows your heart anyway. It's okay to ask God questions because He wants us to be wise. Talk to Him and get whatever you've been holding onto off of your chest. Then come back and, in the space below, write down how you feel and any takeaways you have.

_____

_____

_____

DAY 6

He Understands Our Loneliness

Prayerfully, you were able to be honest with yourself and open with God yesterday. We want to always make sure that we are real with Him because that's a sign that we trust Him, even when it hurts. I just want to spend one more day with you discussing someone else who felt abandoned by God: Jesus Christ. That's right, the fulness of our triune God who became flesh and died so that we can live. The Bible says that God understands every emotion we feel. Jesus was both God and man, and as a man, He had emotions. Therefore it's safe to say that He had experienced loneliness before.

> *Seeing then that we have a great high priest, that is passed into the heavens, Jesus the Son of God, let us hold fast our profession.*
> *For we have not an high priest which cannot be touched with the feeling of our infirmities; but was in all points tempted like as we are, yet without sin.*
>
> Hebrews 4:14-15

Not only does the Bible say that Christ intercedes on our behalf, the Word states that He was tempted in every way we mortal men and women are today. That means He knows just what you're feeling even when you aren't so sure yourself. You may be wondering how Jesus could be lonely when He was God, was always surrounded by people and had the Father on speed dial. Today we'll look at two examples:

1. Jesus in the Garden at Gethsemane
2. Jesus on the cross in Golgotha

Read Matthew 26:36-46.

WEEK TWO

This passage of scripture takes place right before Judas Iscariot arrives with the chief priests to betray Jesus. Let's talk about the background of this passage. It's well-known that Jesus had twelve disciples but out of those twelve, there were three that were always with Him, three that He trusted and spent the most time with: Peter, James and John. James and John were brothers and these three disciples are the ones most often mentioned by name in Scripture. If the twelve were his circle of friends, these three were like Jesus' best friends, the ones He could always depend on. So, of course, it is these three that He chooses to bring to the garden of Gethsemane when He knows that His death is imminent.

Can you imagine knowing when you were about to die? Let alone knowing that it would be a painful and prolonged death. Jesus didn't die quick. He was beaten and tortured for days before He hung on the cross, and He was on that crucifix for a long time. The Messiah knew it would be painful because He knew that His death would be for our sins. That's a lot of sin to cover which meant a lot of blood needed to be shed. I can't begin to imagine the mental anguish out Savior was going through and yet He went through for us. And before He went through all of that, Jesus went to the Father in prayer.

Write Matthew 26:38 in the space below.

_____

_____

Read Mark 14:32-42. What does Jesus say in verse 34?

_____

_____

_____

Sometimes, even as believers, we forget that Jesus was both God and man, which means He had emotions. Jesus was sorrowful even unto death. He prayed in the garden because He knew that He needed the sort of strength only God provides to endure what was necessary to save us from sin and death. There are some battles that we can only survive through the strength of the Lord and Jesus was right in the middle of one.

Record a time you were in a difficult battle and needed the strength of the Lord.

_____

_____

_____

_____

Day 6

It was hard to get through, right? Even though you knew God was there, it was still a struggle. Likewise, it couldn't have been easy to stare death and torment in the face even if Jesus knew He'd win. And so, Jesus asked His three ride-or-die friends to come and just keep Him company while He prayed. But what do they do? They fall asleep. Jesus isn't even gone one hour before He comes and sees them sleeping when they were supposed to be awake and vigilant. The Bible says this happened three times before Judas and the guards came to take Jesus into captivity. Three times! Imagine being let done by those you trust not once, not twice but three times. In the same day! It's an awful feeling. And we cannot forget the dilemma Christ was in, He was praying for His very life.

And being in an agony he prayed more earnestly: and his sweat was as it were great drops of blood falling down to the ground.

Luke 22:44

Christ was in agony, praying so hard and hurting so much that He began to sweat blood (and this is after an angel strengthens Him in verse 43). Plus, the three he trusted and loved so much couldn't even stay awake. Would you have been hurt in this situation? How would you have reacted?

_____
_____
_____
_____
_____
_____

The Bible says that the Spirit in the three men was willing but their flesh was weak, which is why they gave in and fell asleep. In the natural, it's easy to understand: it was late at night, they had just had a big meal, they were in a dark place with nothing to do except keep watch. Some of us couldn't last ten minutes in a similar plight and without the distractions of phones, televisions, books and whatever else, our boredom would lull us to sleep. Jesus knew that the three were trying but still, their best wasn't enough to keep them awake. We've all had times where we feel let down but we must remind ourselves that people are only people, no matter if you've been friends for a decade. Even close friends let you down sometimes. People aren't perfect and even when they're doing their best, they may still fall short because they aren't God. Still, it had to hurt seeing His friends fast asleep while He was feeling tormented.

The Bible also tells of Jesus feeling forsaken by the Heavenly Father.

And at the ninth hour Jesus cried with a loud voice, saying, Eloi, Eloi, lama sabachthani? which is, being interpreted, My God, my God, why hast thou forsaken me?

Mark 15:34

Why is this what Jesus cries out? Well, we know that God is holy and perfect, we know that in Him there is no sin. Psalm 5:4 says that evil (which is sin) can't dwell in God. To put it simply, the two don't mix because one is pure and the other is corrupt. God can't dwell in a sinful person (one who continues to sin without remorse). ***Note: Missing the mark once or twice as you strive for holiness doesn't make you a sinner or a sinful person, it makes you a Christian who's working to be more like Christ.***

While on the Cross, Jesus took on all sin, every sin that was committed and will be committed fell on Him while He was hanging bloody and bruised. In that moment, since Christ bore the weight of our iniquities, God could no longer dwell with Him.

Have you ever felt forsaken by God? Why or why not?

_____

_____

If you had only a few words to describe your mental state at that time, what words would you use?

_____

_____

Jesus, who'd been walking with the Lord, spending hours alone in His presence each day could, all at once, no longer do that. Our Father had to allow Jesus to suffer on that cross alone in order to save us. You might think that He wasn't alone because He had John, Mary and Mary Magdelene there the whole time, but have you ever been separated from someone you love? Whether you had a fight or there was a move or anything similar? Being apart from someone who's a large and influential part of your life creates a void in you and you begin to realize that because of all the time you spent with them, they have, in a way, become a part of your identity. You may have others around but it's just not the same without that person there. Losing that connection is tough to deal with. Jesus lost connection with the one who created Heaven and Earth, His Father, His Teacher. God had to leave because He cannot be in the midst of sin and since Jesus knew the Scriptures, He knew it would happen. Still, knowing and experiencing it are very different things.

Day 6

Not only was Christ forsaken by His friends in His time of need but He didn't even have the presence of the Lord to comfort Him before His death. Have you ever been so mentally downtrodden that you needed help yet when you sought it out, couldn't get it? What happened?

_____
_____
_____
_____
_____
_____
_____
_____
_____

What would you say to someone else in this situation?

_____
_____

Are you willing to take your own advice?

_____
_____

Everyone feels lonely, misunderstood and even unheard at times. It is a consequence of living in this fallen world. These last few days we have gone over quite a lot of examples and I hope they remind you that you're not alone in this. Tomorrow, we will discuss ways to combat the spirits of loneliness and depression so that we can live with a "nevertheless" mindset. Take some time to write out a "nevertheless" statement and post it somewhere you are sure to see it later, like your bathroom mirror or on the back of your bedroom door. Ask God to bring these statements to your memory whenever you feel alone, forgotten or unimportant so that they can encourage you.

DAY 7

Learning the Truth About Who You Are

This week our focus has been on loneliness that stems from feelings of misunderstandings and abandonment. We touched on self-isolation, bitterness, and a few other things. Loneliness is a dangerous emotion. It causes you to pull away from even your closest friends while it makes you think they don't care or that they deserve better friends than you. Likewise, loneliness creates bitterness and hurt that transforms into sin. How? When you are bitter you begin to treat people harshly, you stop forgiving, you begin to regret your past and make even start questioning God or turning away from Him.

> *Looking diligently lest any man fail of the grace of God; lest any root of bitterness springing up trouble you, and thereby many be defiled;*
>
> Hebrews 12:15

Has loneliness ever affected your walk with God? Be honest, detail how it happened below.

_____
_____
_____
_____
_____

Day 7

Loneliness is a natural emotion, but as we studied earlier, emotions lie. They are fleeting and they aren't based on the whole truth of your situation, only a small snippet of how you perceive it. Additionally, while we are living in this natural body, we are spiritual beings. We have to stop thinking naturally because that is the way the world thinks and we are no longer citizens of this world, but citizens of God's kingdom.

Read the following verses and write down the truth of who you are next to them.

- Philippians 3:20-21
- 1 Peter 2:9-10
- 1 Peter 2:4
- John 15:16
- 2 Timothy 1:9
- Jeremiah 1:5

You are chosen and called to do a marvelous work for the Lord. You have purpose and life but when you trust too much in your emotions, these truths about your identity become muddled. You begin to devote all your time to (and I say this with love) feeling sorry for yourself. I've thrown more pity parties that I can count and yes, some of them have been after I was saved. But as I continue to mature in the Lord, they occur less often. I'm trusting less in fleeting feelings and more in the stable foundation that is God and His Word. And that is what we have to focus on. God is the great I AM, He is unchanging and eternal. As believers, we've been told time and time again that His Word is true but do you believe it? And, if so, do you always believe in that truth or only when it's easy or convenient?

_____

_____

_____

I decided that while writing this study, I would be as transparent as I have asked you to be. I'm answering the questions I pose and am facing some things I thought I had moved past. Loneliness is one of them. As a child, I always felt unbearably alone. Everyone seemed to fit in except me, it felt like no one in my family truly wanted me around and so, to make it easier on them, I stopped coming around. They went to dinners and parks and I stayed home. All that time, I felt unwanted and forgotten. I felt like my entire existence was a burden and that everyone around would be happier if I wasn't there. And this loneliness led me to put on a mask. I stopped showing how I really felt and just decided to blend in with everyone, even if I didn't actually like them. It also led to a deep resentment of everyone around me. I wondered why no one seemed to notice the change, no one seemed to want to know the real me. Why couldn't I stay happy? Why had the world kept moving when it felt like I was falling into a black hole? You can imagine how these bitter emotions led me away from the good God that created me and knew me before I was even born. But now, I am thankful for those years and that experience because it allows me to understand others going through the same battle.

Has loneliness ever caused you to sin? What happened?

_____

_____

Have you asked for forgiveness? Is so, thank God for His mercy and if not, take time to do so.

_____

_____

Loneliness is dangerous and while everyone may feel it at one time or another, we cannot allow it to consume us or else we risk our relationship with our Father. So today, on the final day of this week's study, we will work out strategies to combat and defeat it.

Read the Word.

Over the course of this week, I hope that there have been some scriptures that resonated with your spirit. The Word is living and has a solution for every issue we face. When you feel alone or confused about anything in the world, you can go to God's Word and find a story or principle that can motivate you to keep going when the odds are stacked against you.

Write a verse that you connected with this week below.

_____

_____

Additionally, since we know that emotions lie and cloud are judgement, we have to come against the lies with truth. And there is no greater truth than the Word. It is one of the ways the Lord speaks to us and even when dealing with familiar passages, you may be surprised with new revelation from the Holy Spirit. That same old Bible verse you learned in children's church twenty years ago may be the verse that breaks your chains and sets you free.

Below, write a verse that encourages you, one that we did not discuss.

_____

_____

Day 7

Get in the presence of God.

The world is distracting. Everything in the media is about who you should be and how to achieve it, media is one of the biggest factors in loneliness because it causes us to feel we're lacking some crucial component and that without it we can never have joy. With all of that noise coming in, it can be hard to think clearly. In these times, we must go to God and come to Him honestly. Tell the Lord about what you're dealing with. If you're sad or angry or bitter, let Him know. You don't have to sugarcoat anything or pretend like it isn't important or laugh it off. God loves honest, He wants us to be open and vulnerable because it shows that we trust Him.

Write down three things you are dealing with that you need to go to the Father for:

_____

Unless you release everything, you will always have something holding you back and keeping you from moving forward with your life. Think of His presence as medication when you have an infection. We've all been sick and it makes it hard to do normal everyday things. What happens when you don't take all of your medicine, even after specific instruction from your doctor? While you aren't as sick as you were, you aren't completely healthy either. You can get by but you're not living up to your potential because some of that sickness is still within you and it's because you *chose* not to get it all out. Sadly, this means that the next time a similar problem occurs (that infection), the medicine won't work as well because you allowed the sickness to take root in you and grow stronger. Now you have to put in more work than you anticipated and the battle is more grueling then you thought, plus it lasts longer. Getting into God's presence, being alone with Him and just talking with Him is the best prescription anyone could ever offer you. The best part is that it works for any and every sickness.

Fellowship.

When we feel alone, sometimes the hardest thing for us to do is to get in the presence of other believers. The keyword here is believers. When you are dealing with a spiritual battle, you have to surround yourself with other soldiers. Even though you may have some unsaved friends that give great advice, the advice they give would be worldly because that's all they have to offer. But the Word tells us to surround ourselves with wise counsel (Proverbs 24:6) and those who are in the world aren't wise according to the Scriptures; if they were, they wouldn't be in the world. As it says in Luke 6:39, when the blind lead the blind, they both fall in a ditch,

> *And he spake a parable unto them, Can the blind lead the blind? shall they not both fall into the ditch?*
>
> Luke 6:39

WEEK TWO

Write down three godly people you can fellowship with.

And if you don't have three people, pray and ask God for people to fellowship with. And don't be afraid to be specific.

Now, I know that not everyone has a wide circle of godly counselors or friends they can turn to. For me, this is what made fellowship so hard. I was too shy and too scared to seek out new friends even when I began separating myself from my worldly ones. But the Bible says that we have to spend time with other believers if we want to have the strength to keep running this spiritual race.

Take some time and think about ways to make new friends. If you're young but your church doesn't have a youth ministry, find one that does and attend their youth services. Reach out to someone more mature in the faith and ask for counsel. It may be a bit scary or nerve-wracking, but it will help you in the long run. I promise.

Now that we've concluded this week's session, take some time to think on these truths. Hide them in your heart.

- I may feel lonely Nevertheless I am never alone.
- I may feel lonely Nevertheless emotions lie.
- I may feel lonely Nevertheless I will have victory over this situation.
- I may feel lonely Nevertheless God is always with me.

Week Three

I Feel Anxious Nevertheless I Have The Peace Of God

DAY 1

What Is Worry?

*T*hank you for sticking with me through this study! Now that we're halfway to the end, I want to give you a chance to acknowledge your own growth. If you feel as though this study has helped you in any way, write down how below. Then write why you believe you've changed.

_____

_____

As you may have guessed by the title of this week's lesson, we're going to be focusing on anxiety and worry. We've already talked about some rough topics and I've asked you to be open. This week your goal should be to clean up the dirt you may have swept under the rug and move past living with a spirit of anxiety and worry. Worry leads to fear and the Bible says that God didn't give us a spirit of fear, He gives us peace that surpasses all understanding.

> *For God hath not given us the spirit of fear; but of power, and of love, and of a sound mind.*
>
> 2 Timothy 1:7

> *Be careful for nothing; but in every thing by prayer and supplication with thanksgiving let your requests be made known unto God.*
>
> *And the peace of God, which passeth all understanding, shall keep your hearts and minds through Christ Jesus.*
>
> Philippians 4:6-7

These are scriptures commonly heard in church. You may post them on social media or even have them hanging in your house, but do you truly believe them? Do you truly believe you have access to God's peace or does it feel like more of a happy thought, wishful thinking to encourage us in hard times but nothing more? I'll tell you what, I used to think that way. In fact, I felt that way for most of my life but then I began to understand the truth of who God is. God doesn't lie nor does He seek to placate His people with catchy hashtags or sayings. And if God said it, we can have it. While I understood this, I struggled with the concept that God meant for me to have it. The way my life was going, these words were too good to be true so I distanced myself from them. And while I could encourage others, I never thought I could have access to His peace or a sound, worry-free mind.

People today worry about everything from their outfits to their families to even their finances. And while all these things are important, we must learn as believers that worrying about something is not the same as caring about something. We all have things that are important to us and mean a lot but just because I care about these things doesn't mean I should miss meals or lose sleep because I am anxious over them. I don't know anyone who can say they didn't let stress get the better of them at least once so, if I'm hitting home, don't think you're alone in this or that you're a failure of a believer or as a person. You aren't. You are going through a spiritual battle and I've come to remind you that you are going through it. You won't be stuck there.

On that note, I want to stress this point today and throughout the rest of this week: worrying does not equal caring.

Write 5 things you are anxious about and why.

1. _____
2. _____
3. _____
4. _____
5. _____

Now, are the five things you listed above important to you? If even one of them is, you'll be able to follow along. I'll use finances for an example. There are a lot of people who worry about money. Whether it is because of debt, bills or unfair wages people tend to worry about their finances. And money is important because the Bible says it answers all things (Ecclesiastes 10:19). Money, in itself, is a good thing. We are told to be good stewards of it, to handle it responsibly. This is where the disconnect happens. We want to be good stewards and so we try to make wise and rational decisions but often that turns into worry. **Worry is when you feel unease, it happens when you allow yourself to dwell on difficulty or troubles.** You may be going through financial difficulties but when you dwell on them, that is when you begin to grow anxious. Anxiety presents itself in a number of ways. You might start pinching pennies or living beneath your means or maybe you try to earn more money as fast as you can or you may just stop, give in to doubt and cease trying altogether. This isn't only true when talking about money either. Everyone expresses their anxiety differently.

How do you express your anxiety?

_____
_____
_____
_____
_____

Anxiety, worry, distress, whatever you like to call it, is a hindrance to our growth both in the natural and in the spiritual. It leads to doubt and fear and the Word tells us that neither are godly. And God, being good, gives us advice on dealing with these emotions.

Read the scriptures below and write what they mean to you personally.

- John 14:1
- John 14:27
- Isaiah 41:10
- John 4:18
- Psalm 27:1

God knows that worry will attack His people and consistently tells us not to worry. Why? Because worry keeps us from trusting God fully. If we do not trust Him we cannot live the life He has called us to live. Worry keeps us from our purpose. Moreover, worry loves company. When you're worried, before you know it, you'll start pulling others in and then they can't progress in their walk with God either. Sounds pretty dangerous, right? Luckily, there is no enemy that can defeat our God. As we close, take time to address those five things you're anxious about. Pray over them and ask God to help you move past the doubt and fear. Pray that the Lord teaches you how to overcome these situations.

DAY 2

Why We Should Be Anxious For Nothing

We ended yesterday with a brief introduction to worry and what path worry ultimately leads us to. Have you ever let anxiety stop you from doing something? Write the circumstances below.

_____

_____

_____

_____

_____

Let's jump right in and discuss a few of the reasons we shouldn't worry or be anxious as followers of the Lord Jesus Christ. Read Psalm 91 in whatever version you're comfortable with. I have placed it below in the King James. Feel free to take notes in the margin.

> He that dwelleth in the secret place of the most High shall abide under the shadow of the Almighty.
> I will say of the Lord, He is my refuge and my fortress: my God; in him will I trust.
> Surely he shall deliver thee from the snare of the fowler, and from the noisome pestilence.
> He shall cover thee with his feathers, and under his wings shalt thou trust: his truth shall be thy shield and buckler.

Thou shalt not be afraid for the terror by night; nor for the arrow that flieth by day;
Nor for the pestilence that walketh in darkness; nor for the destruction that wasteth at noonday.
A thousand shall fall at thy side, and ten thousand at thy right hand; but it shall not come nigh thee.
Only with thine eyes shalt thou behold and see the reward of the wicked.
Because thou hast made the Lord, which is my refuge, even the most High, thy habitation;
There shall no evil befall thee, neither shall any plague come nigh thy dwelling.
For he shall give his angels charge over thee, to keep thee in all thy ways.
They shall bear thee up in their hands, lest thou dash thy foot against a stone.
Thou shalt tread upon the lion and adder: the young lion and the dragon shalt thou trample under feet.
Because he hath set his love upon me, therefore will I deliver him: I will set him on high, because he hath known my name.
He shall call upon me, and I will answer him: I will be with him in trouble; I will deliver him, and honour him.
With long life will I satisfy him, and shew him my salvation.

That's a pretty amazing promise, isn't it? God promises to keep His people and that leads us to reason number one of why we shouldn't be anxious.

1. God is our protector.

The Word of God tells us that we'll be persecuted, that life won't always be easy. Many believers forget this part. We forget that trials and tribulations will come so we aren't as prepared as we should be when they occur. How do we get prepared? By being in a close relationship with God and having our armor on. Still, even with the armor we need God to protect us and, as it says in Psalm 91, He will even when we're surrounded on all sides and ready to give into defeat.

Read 2 Kings 6:1-17.

Elisha's servant seemed right to be afraid, they were surrounded by the army of an angry king. The Bible says it was a great host. It wasn't just a few dozen men, this was an entire army sent to bring Elisha to the king. Can you imagine going up against an entire army by yourself? I sure can't. But for some reason, Elisha was calm.

Write 2 Kings 6:16 in the space below.

_____

_____

_____

Not only was Elisha at ease but he even tells his servant to remain calm. There were only two of them against the king's men and yet Elisha said that they had more than the king's great host. And he was right! Once the young servant's spiritual eyes were opened, he could see what Elisha saw, that God had sent an even greater host to protect them. Just because we cannot always see God moving on our behalf doesn't mean He isn't moving. God protects His people and since we know He isn't a respecter of person, we know He protects us all, regardless of our titles, ministry, wealth or anything else the world uses to divide people. So, the next time you're worried and feel like giving up is your only choice, thank God for the angels He's sent to protect you.

2. God is our provider.

One reason people tend it worry is provision. We are always in need of various resources to go about our daily lives and when we feel as though the resources we desire aren't available, we begin to panic.

Read 1 Kings 17:7-16.

In Biblical times, widows lived a hard life. Remember what I said earlier in the study? Women couldn't work in most vocations and when they did make money, they earned very little. That being said, this story takes place in the middle of a drought, which means there was little food to eat as no water means poor harvests. The Lord told Elijah to go to Zarepheith and that a widow would sustain him there. We see in the passage that while the widow was willing to give Elijah water, she had little food to offer. In fact, she had been planning on dressing up some meal for her and her son and dying. This woman had no hope because she had no food. Understandable but get this, even though she had no food, she still obeyed the man of God.

Reread verses 14-16.

How long were they all able to eat off her meal?

_____

But my God shall supply all your need according to his riches in glory by Christ Jesus.
Philippians 4:19

How many of your needs will God meet?

_____

_____

Day 2

How has God met your needs before?

_____
_____
_____
_____
_____
_____
_____
_____
_____
_____

That's right, the Lord will meet all of our needs, just as He met the needs of the widow and her child. If you have a little and God, you have more than enough. God will provide because He is our source. We can get everything we need if we just go to Him and ask.

Do you have a need you want God to meet? Use the space below to ask God for in faith. Lay it at His feet and don't pick it up again.

_____
_____
_____

3. God knows us.

Anxiety has no room in your heart, it shouldn't exist there and one of the big reasons why it shouldn't is because God knows us. You might be wondering what that has to do with not being anxious and I get it, it isn't as cut and dry as the first two reasons. But I want you to open up your heart and mind to this concept.

God knows us, He knows every single detail about us and He knows more about us than we even know ourselves. Don't you think this same God knows what you need, when you need it and how you should use it? Don't you think the God who knows you and takes care of you, knew how you would react to this situation and gave you a way to get out. The Father never leaves us trapped in our dilemma. He always gives us a way out but sometimes we can't see the door clearly because worry has fogged our eyes.

There hath no temptation taken you but such as is common to man: but God is faithful, who will not suffer you to be tempted above that ye are able; but will with the temptation also make a way to escape, that ye may be able to bear it.

1 Corinthians 10:13

For each and every dilemma, there is a way out. Your way out may look different than someone else's and that is because the Father tailored it specifically for you. He knows exactly how much you can bear and what you can handle.

Yea, though I walk through the valley of the shadow of death, I will fear no evil: for thou art with me; thy rod and thy staff they comfort me.

Psalm 23:4

Now go back and highlight or underline the word "through." Do the same with the phrases "fear no evil," "art with me" and "comfort me." Once you realize just how personal our God is, you will begin to understand that He'll bring you through your circumstances. That means you'll get out of it and because we know the outcome, we don't have to worry about the battle.

There are other reasons why we don't have to feel anxious, all with examples in the Word but I wanted to share these three specifically with you and I hope they make you think. Use the space below to write out how these three key notes can help you move past the worries you listed yesterday.

_____
_____
_____
_____
_____
_____
_____
_____
_____

DAY 3

The Difference Between Care And Worry

For most people, the line between caring and worrying is very thin, so how can we avoid crossing it? Today, I want you to think about how you can prevent yourself from worrying no matter how deeply you care about something or how important it may be. Worry happens when we shift our focus and lose sight of what is really important: God. We may not say it or even think it but in our hearts, we begin to allow "it," whatever "it" is, to take precedence over spending time with God.

> Now it came to pass, as they went, that he entered into a certain village: and a certain woman named Martha received him into her house.
> And she had a sister called Mary, which also sat at Jesus' feet, and heard his word.
> But Martha was cumbered about much serving, and came to him, and said, Lord, dost thou not care that my sister hath left me to serve alone? bid her therefore that she help me.
> And Jesus answered and said unto her, Martha, Martha, thou art careful and troubled about many things:
> But one thing is needful: and Mary hath chosen that good part, which shall not be taken away from her.
>
> Luke 10:38-42

Let me give you some background on this fairly short story. Mary and Martha are the sisters of Lazarus. Yep, the same Lazarus that was Jesus' friend, the man He rose from the dead with just the words from His lips. Feel free to read that story in John 11:1-44. Now, in John 11:5, the

Bible says that Jesus loved the three siblings. Isn't it wonderful to be loved by God? Anyway, the siblings weren't strangers to Jesus and they knew that He was more than just a wise man. They knew that Jesus was sent directly from the Father and Jesus was a welcome guest in their home. What do you do when you have guests? You make sure they are comfortable and well-taken care of. And wouldn't you work that much harder if the Son of Man decided to pop up and sit on your couch for a while?

Be open and honest. How would you react if Jesus, in the flesh, decided He wanted to hang out at your house? What would you do for Him? Would you feel nervous? Uncomfortable? Jot down your thoughts as they come to mind.

_____
_____
_____
_____
_____

Do you think wanting to care for you guests makes you a bad person?

_____

Then why is it that so many believers look down on Martha's actions?

_____
_____
_____
_____

Look at verse 40 again. The King James Version says that she was "cumbered about much serving." The New International Version says she was "distracted by all the preparations that had to be made." Consistently, the Bible tells us to treat others well and to be prepared so wasn't Martha just doing what she thought was right? Yes, she was. Hospitality was extremely important at that time. How you treated your guests showed where your heart was, it was a testament of your character. Martha merely wanted to make a good impression. There is absolutely nothing wrong with her intentions. The trouble rises when she allows herself to be distracted. A distraction is something

Day 3

that keeps us from giving our full attention to something else. Distractions leave us unable to concentrate because our mind is too preoccupied.

Have you ever been distracted and it pulled you away from something important?

_____

Have you ever been distracted by something that seemed pretty important?

_____

Did that distraction cause you to feel stressed or anxious?

_____

That is exactly how Martha was feeling. She had to feed her sister, Jesus and His disciples. All she wanted was a little help because the stress was getting to be too much for her. Write how Jesus responds to Martha's request below:

_____

_____

_____

Jesus first lets Martha know that He sees her efforts and understands how she feels. Then He tells her that while the things she was doing were important, there was only one needful thing, one good part: to sit at the feet of Jesus, to be intimate with Him. Jesus knows what we go through, He knows what we worry about and why but no matter how important those things are, He tells us to never lose sight of the most important aspect of our lives: having a close relationship with the triune God.

Is there something in your life distracting you from spending quality time with God?

_____

Why is it taking priority in your life?

___

The Father constantly warns against losing sight of Him among the never-ending noise of our everyday lives. He tells the church of Ephesus in Revelation 2:4 that they have stopping putting Him first, so even though they are doing everything else right, He holds it against them. In verse five of that chapter, God tells the church to repent. Below, I have left some space for you to ask God the Father to forgive you. If you have lost sight of what's important, if you've left your first love, if you've been putting God on the backburner, speak to Him. Be real with Him. Tell Him what it is and why. Ask both for forgiveness and for a mind and heart to do better in the future.

DAY 4

Worry And Coping

Be careful for nothing; but in every thing by prayer and supplication with thanksgiving let your requests be made known unto God.

And the peace of God, which passeth all understanding, shall keep your hearts and minds through Christ Jesus.

Philippians 4:6-7

Take a good look at verse six. It says to not be careful, to not be anxious or stressed or worried about anything. For so long, this seemed like an ideal to me, an impossible dream that I could never achieve. I was a big worrywart and a lot of that stemmed from caution. I wanted to keep all of my bases covered so that even if things didn't go as planned, I would be no worse off then when I started. I purposefully held low expectations for every aspect of my life because I believed that lower expectations meant a lower chance of being disappointed. My entire existence was surrounded by bright yellow caution tape.

Do you ever feel overly cautious? What about? I shared my coping mechanism with you, what's yours?

_____

_____

_____

_____

WEEK THREE

Even if you are still battling with this struggle, we are going to speak to those things that aren't as though they are and declare your victory over this issue.

In the space below, write out some affirmations or statements to help remind you not to worry.

_____

_____

_____

Sometimes caution is good, we are to approach life with wisdom. This wisdom tells us not to take a shortcut through a sketchy alley, to be mindful of what we say, to tread carefully on ice. When caution comes from a place of wisdom, you are doing well but what about when it comes from a place of fear?

Read Matthew 25:14-30.

What did the servants get and what did they give back to their master?

_____

_____

The third servant is the only one who gave back the exact amount of money he'd been given before the master went away. Verse 25 tells us why the servant hid the money, he was afraid. He was afraid and his fear led him to hide what he was given rather than make use of it. The master even says that if he was afraid, he could've given the money to the exchangers so that the master could earn a bit of interest. There is a lot of truth in this proverb, but I wish to focus on the precaution the third servant took and the final result of said caution.

The servant was afraid and so, instead of using caution that comes from wisdom and earning interest on it (even if he didn't trade it), the servant used caution that stemmed from fear. Verse 15 states that the master gave to the servants according to their ability which means that each servant got the exact amount they could handle, no more, no less. But although the servant was capable enough to handle it, he let fear take over and in the end he ended up with less than what he had at the beginning.

> *You have more than enough to handle everything God has given you.*

Day 4

Reread verses 28-30 and write down everything that happens to the unprofitable servant.

_____

I know that a lot people read the last few verses of this parable and think it's a harsh punishment, it's not like the master is any worse off, right? But think of it this way, if you let worry and fear keep you from doing a little, how could you ever handle more? Yes, the servant knew that his master was strict and so he wanted to make sure he didn't lose it but in digging a hole and burying his talent of silver in the ground, he showed the master that he would allow worry to stop him from doing anything profitable.

As believers, we are called to be profitable for the kingdom, to make disciples and share the faith but worry won't allow us to do that. Have you ever missed an opportunity to do something on God's behalf? Why is that? Were you being overly cautious?

_____

Write down three times in your life that you let caution stemming from fear hinder your spiritual growth. Then write how you could have used caution that comes from wisdom in those same situations.

_____

Now rewrite Philippians 4:6-7 in your own words.

Take this passage with you and think on it throughout the week. Has your idea of this passage changed over the course of this week's lesson?

DAY 5

Anxiety Over The Future

But what if? How many times have you asked yourself that question? Have you ever sat around thinking about all the possible scenarios that could play out? As humans, we tend to be curious, we like knowing what's coming around the corner. And when we can't get a clear picture, we tend to make things up. We come up with all kinds of possibilities, we make up conversations in our heads and try to imagine how others would react when we say or do certain things. But maybe it's just me. I think about the future quite a lot and I used to worry about it just as often. I'm not perfect but I am progressing, just as you are. We are all in this together so it's okay to admit that you are worried about all of the possible outcomes. But the Lord tells us not to worry about tomorrow because tomorrow will worry about itself. Read the passage below and be sure to mark things that stick out to you.

Matthew 6:25-34 King James Version (KJV)
Therefore I say unto you, Take no thought for your life, what ye shall eat, or what ye shall drink; nor yet for your body, what ye shall put on. Is not the life more than meat, and the body than raiment?

Behold the fowls of the air: for they sow not, neither do they reap, nor gather into barns; yet your heavenly Father feedeth them. Are ye not much better than they?

Which of you by taking thought can add one cubit unto his stature?

And why take ye thought for raiment? Consider the lilies of the field, how they grow; they toil not, neither do they spin:

And yet I say unto you, That even Solomon in all his glory was not arrayed like one of these.

Wherefore, if God so clothe the grass of the field, which to day is, and to morrow is cast into the oven, shall he not much more clothe you, O ye of little faith?

Therefore take no thought, saying, What shall we eat? or, What shall we drink? or, Wherewithal shall we be clothed?

(For after all these things do the Gentiles seek:) for your heavenly Father knoweth that ye have need of all these things.

But seek ye first the kingdom of God, and his righteousness; and all these things shall be added unto you.

Take therefore no thought for the morrow: for the morrow shall take thought for the things of itself. Sufficient unto the day is the evil thereof.

The NIV translation puts verse 34 this way:

Therefore do not worry about tomorrow, for tomorrow will worry about itself. Each day has enough trouble of its own.

There's enough trouble in the day you are in now so why are you piling more onto your plate? We only increase our stress when we worry about things that haven't happened yet. Jesus is telling us that there is no reason to make things harder for yourself than they already are. And yet, sometimes it feels like we just can't help it, like we are somehow hardwired to worry. We pace the floor and lie awake at night because we just can't help ourselves. I want you to know that is not the case. We don't have to stress about the future or worry about how we'll make it out of this one. Worry is not a prerequisite for being human and God Himself tells us that we shouldn't waste time doing it.

Have you ever felt like you just had to worry about something?

_____

_____

Write a note to yourself below, to remind you not to worry about the future.

_____

_____

_____

_____

I hope that you memorize what you just wrote and take it to heart so that the next time you begin to worry you already have a plan of attack.

What causes us to worry about things that haven't happened yet as well as things that will most likely never happen? Uncertainty. The enemy wants us to believe that we have to know everything, that we have to be in control over everything, that we make our own destiny. When we feel as though we are in complete control over our circumstances we leave God out of the picture. Isn't that how the serpent tricked Eve in the Garden? He told her that she would have knowledge and be like God by eating the fruit and the idea of being like God was so tempting that she forgot she was already like the Father and took a bite (Genesis 3:1-6). Knowledge is important. The Bible reminds us of this so often because so that we can accept it as truth. We cannot allow the enemy, the world or even our own flesh to twist the hunger for knowledge (which is good) into anxiety over uncertain circumstance (which is unlike God).

Do you remember the story of Moses? Well, like many of us today, Moses had a lot of "what ifs" running around in his mind and he was so afraid of the unknown that if it had truly been up to him, there is no doubt in my mind that he wouldn't have led Israel anywhere, he would've stayed in Midian tending to his father-in-law's sheep.

Read Exodus 3:6-14 and Exodus 4:1-17.

Below write every excuse Moses made as to why he couldn't deliver the Israelites out of the hands of the Egyptians. Next to each excuse, write how the Lord responded.

_____

_____

_____

_____

_____

_____

_____

_____

_____

_____

_____

All of the excuses that Moses gives make sense…to him. To him, they are valid reasons as to why he can't be of use to God. Let's not forget the major one that isn't mentioned in the verses I gave you: Moses was a murderer on the run. True, Moses was a murderer, a nobody, he didn't know what to say or how to say it, he figured the Israelites would never believe him and he had a speech impediment. In his own eyes, Moses wasn't cut out to be a leader. What excuses have you been giving God lately?

_____
_____
_____
_____
_____

Why?

_____
_____
_____
_____
_____

Let's look at Exodus 4:1 again. Moses tells the Lord that the people won't believe him or listen to what he has to say. Moses even tells the Lord what the people will say. Doesn't this sound like what we talked about earlier? Creating conversations and coming up with how people will respond in a situation that hasn't even happened?

Have you ever done this? Did the conversation end up taking place? Did it turn out exactly as you imagined it?

_____
_____
_____

There's no merit in worrying about the future because we can never know the future. Besides, the majority of the time, the things we stress over never happen.

Have you ever spent time worrying about something that never happened?

_____
_____

Day 5

Time is precious. Our time on this planet is limited and we don't know how much time we have so why are you using such a precious commodity worrying about the "what ifs" of life? What did Jesus say back in Matthew 6:34? Tomorrow is when you need to be thinking about tomorrow. Moses came up with excuse after excuse and not one of them dealt with things God couldn't touch. We stress and freak out over possibilities instead of remembering that when you give it to God He'll never lead you astray. So today, let the Lord handle what will happen tomorrow and the tomorrow after that too. Stop making yourself sick over the future, live in and rejoice in the now. You can do it. I believe in you. And guess what? So does God. That's why He called you.

DAY 6

Anxiety Over The Past

Dealing with the future is one thing but we can't forget to talk about the past. This session will deal with being anxious over past situations, those old arguments and embarrassments that don't want to leave us alone. Holding onto the past often causes us to miss out on the good God has for us in the present.

Read 2 Samuel 9.

Mephibosheth, in my opinion, is one of the most interesting people in the Bible. He was the son of Jonathan (King Saul's son) and he was lame. During the time that this story takes place, it was common practice that when a new king took over, he would kill all the relatives of the previous one so that nobody could one day raise and lay claim to the throne. Since, this was so common, once word spread that David had killed Saul, those related to him all began to flee. This was true of Jonathan's household as well, even though Jonathan and David had been good friends (although Jonathan is dead by this point in the story). Mephibosheth was a young child when his family began to run for their lives and somehow, in all of the hysteria, his nursemaid dropped him and from then on he could no longer walk. Years went by before David got around to showing kindness to Jonathan's family and by this point, poor Mephibosheth was staying in Lo-debar. Lo-debar was a pretty awful place. It was a town of forgotten people, people who had little or nothing at all. Lo-debar literally means "without pasture;" it was a place without refuge and without hope. Mephibosheth was royalty and yet he was living is such a place.

Have you ever been in a spiritual Lo-debar?

_____

_____

Day 6

How did you feel at that time?

_____

_____

_____

Did you forget that you were royalty while you were there?

_____

_____

Mephibosheth was called by King David and he was rightfully afraid. By all means, the man before him could kill him and no one would bat an eye. But David tells him to not be afraid and he vows to be kind to him for Jonathan's sake. Understandably, Mephibosheth finds it hard to believe. He calls himself a servant and a dead dog. He didn't think he was worthy of such kind treatment because of his history. He was crippled in both feet and his grandfather had tried time and time again to kill David. He thought his past disqualified him from being happy in the present but that was not the case.

Reread verses 9 through 13 and write down below all the good things that happened to Mephibosheth and his family.

_____

_____

_____

_____

_____

The King James Version (KJV) ends this part of Mephibosheth's story by noting that the man was still lame in both feet even as he lived well and sat at the king's table. What he'd experienced didn't take him out of the running to live a happy and peaceful life. Likewise, your past, no matter what happened to you or what you did, is in the past. Don't allow it to dictate how you live in the present. Even after David told Mephibosheth the good plans he had for him, the young man countered with "but I'm not worthy." He saw himself as wretched. He'd gone from royalty to being lame to living in a place of hopelessness for the majority of his life. He doubted anything good was even possible for him.

Have you ever been so distraught by something that happened in your past that you thought you didn't deserve anything good in the present? Write down what happened and how you overcame. And if you are still in the middle of this particular battle, ask God to help you get through and help you focus on the good He has in store.

_____

_____

_____

_____

_____

_____

_____

_____

Do you think on past conversations and arguments and wonder how they could have been different? Have thoughts of "woulda, coulda, shoulda?" I do too. I wonder if life would be different or better if I did A instead of B, if I befriended this person instead of that person, if I said this after he or she had said that. And you know how that sort of thinking makes me feel? Annoyed, regretful, upset and empty. Those aren't nice emotions, they're the kind of negativity that keeps you from living in the present and walking in your purpose. Think of it this way, you can't move forward if you're always looking behind you. And if you try, you're bound to stumble and fall. That's the truth of the matter. It's blunt and it isn't all that pretty, but it is the truth. If you ever want to grow, you have to leave the past behind you. This doesn't mean forget it, it's not like Mephibosheth suddenly began walking, it means to stop wallowing on what could have been. You can't change the past and you shouldn't want to. If you hadn't gone through that storm or had that tough conversation you wouldn't be who you are today. And you should love who you are because God does. Take that with you today and share it with someone else.

DAY 7

Let's Be Real, How Do We Combat Anxiety?

Be careful for nothing; but in every thing by prayer and supplication with thanksgiving let your requests be made known unto God.
And the peace of God, which passeth all understanding, shall keep your hearts and minds through Christ Jesus.

Philippians 4:6-7

This week we dealt with worry and a few of its many forms. My prayer for you is that as you grow in God, worry flees your heart. I pray that anxiety vanishes and that you can say you truly have the peace of God in your heart. Today, I want to go over a few ways to fight worry because just knowing why you're anxious doesn't always help. Furthermore, I want every lesson in this book to be applicable to daily life. The knowledge is good but if you cannot apply it you can never grow.

Peace is the opposite of worry and anxiety, right? We also know that Jesus is the Prince of Peace and that the Holy Spirit is the Comforter but how do we use the Word of God to combat worry?

1. Speak God's Promises Over Your Life.

The Word is full of God's promises to us. They aren't just for other people, they are for you! The Bible is living and if He said something back then, it is still true today. Read the following verses and write down the promise God made to you in each one.

Isaiah 41:10
Isaiah 43:2
James 1:5
Deuteronomy 31:8
Jeremiah 29:11
John 8:36
Psalm 34:17
Romans 8:38

When we speak the promises of God, when we meditate on them and trust that His word is true, we begin to see change in our lives. Pick one verse that really speaks to you from the above list. I challenge you to repeat that verse twice a day for a week. See how your attitude towards your situation changes. In fact, take as many verses as you want. There's power in your words so when you consistently say something you begin to believe it, whether what you're saying is good or bad. Stop speaking death, sickness and unhappiness over your life. Speak the good, even if you can't see any good around. The Bible says in Romans 4:17 that we can speak those things that aren't as though they were.

Below write three things you want to see happen in your life.

1. _____
2. _____
3. _____

I urge you to speak these things daily.

2. Listen To Worship Music.

When you were in the world and felt sad, what kind of music did you turn on? For me, the worse I felt, the sadder the music. I don't even understand it but it made sense to me at the time. I was sad and the song was sad, we were in the same boat. But as I matured I realized that those songs were only making me feel worse; they were keeping me miserable. And I would get so miserable, anxious and fearful that I couldn't do anything.

Have you ever felt like that?

When you stress over your situation, your first response should be to worship. When you're in the presence of God, there's no room for fear or doubt because His peace is there. Listen to a few worship songs that acknowledge the goodness of God, no matter how awful your situation may be, you'll be encouraged. You may think that a song couldn't do much but when I face hard times, worship gets me through. I recall being in college and struggling because I was a double

Day 7

major. My favorite uncle was in the final stages of cancer in my hometown a thousand miles away, my friend group split and I was having trouble affording tuition and wondering if I should drop out. I thought about it but my uncle had promised me that he would live to see me graduate that upcoming spring, so I stayed in school. There was a lot on my plate and since I always let others push their issues on me, soon my plate was overflowing and beginning to crack under the weight. But that Sunday, I went to church, hoping for a God experience and the worship team came up and sang a song that changed my life. If you've ever heard "When You Walk Into the Room" by Bryan and Katie Towalt, you know just how powerful the lyrics are. To this day, I listen to it when I feel stuck or unsure because, as the song says, in God's presence "every hopeless situation ceases to exist."

Take some time to listen to a worship song. Write a few lyrics that resonate with you below.

_____

_____

_____

3. Step Away.

Have you ever felt as though if you didn't do something it would never get done? That you had to prepare for every possible outcome, just in case? We allow stress to enter in and one of the easiest ways to get rid of it can, for many, be the hardest. And that is to step away. Relaxing and taking breaks is okay. Sometimes you have to remove yourself from a situation, if only for a little while. I don't know about you but I would get so anxious over things I had no control over and even things that didn't have anything to do with me, but I didn't want to release those things. I thought that if I wasn't stressed on my friends' behalf then I wasn't a good friend, that to be an adult is to be stressed but not letting it ruin your productivity. But that isn't what God has for us. He says to be careful in nothing.

Write down below something you need to step away from and something you can do to relax.

_____

_____

_____

_____

4. Stop Worrying And Let Go.

Write 3 situations or things that cause you stress that you will let go of.

1. _____
2. _____
3. _____

Why were you holding onto these things?

_____

Worry is not of God. He didn't give us a spirit of fear, in fact, He gave us the opposite: a sound mind. A mind that is steady, determined and able to handle whatever comes our way. As we end this week, think on who you are and who you could be if you release the worry and anxiety in your life. Think about your main causes of worry and pray that God becomes more important to you than your current situation.

Week Four

Mental, Emotional & Physical Exhaustion

DAY 1

Are You Sick And Tired Of Being Sick And Tired?

We've made it to the last week of our study! We've talked about fear, feelings of inferiority, anxiety and how God is in the midst of all these emotions and how He still has plans for you. I hope that in the last three weeks, you've learned something that helps you walk through this life that can be so trying at times. And that is what this week is about, feeling like you want to give up because you're just tired.

Have you ever been sick and tired of being sick and tired?

_____

What was the cause? What did you do?

_____

_____

_____

_____

Whether it is emotionally, mentally or physically, we've all been there. We've all felt worn down or so tired that we didn't want to continue. This week we'll look at men and women who felt the same way but at the end of this study, I hope you'll be able to say "I'm tired nevertheless, God is on my side and I can keep going."

Isaiah 40:28-31 King James Version (KJV)
Hast thou not known? hast thou not heard, that the everlasting God, the Lord, the Creator of the ends of the earth, fainteth not, neither is weary? there is no searching of his understanding.
He giveth power to the faint; and to them that have no might he increaseth strength.
Even the youths shall faint and be weary, and the young men shall utterly fall:
But they that wait upon the Lord shall renew their strength; they shall mount up with wings as eagles; they shall run, and not be weary; and they shall walk, and not faint.

This chapter in the Bible lets us know that everyone gets weary at one point or another. Isaiah 40 is God speaking to the people of Israel and offering them comfort. They were tired and by this time, they had every right to be. Israel was going through a lot. They wanted to give up, throw in the towel and say, "Enough is enough." But God never gets tired and He gives power to the faint. Because we have God on our side we can keep going, we have the strength to keep moving even though we may feel exhausted.

For I have satiated the weary soul, and I have replenished every sorrowful soul.
Jeremiah 31:25

Read Matthew 11:25-30.

What do these verses mean to you?

_____

_____

_____

We all have a burden on our shoulders and God wants to take that burden from us. He says in verse 30 that His yoke is easy and His burden is light. That doesn't mean that we won't have a burden to bear but that it'll be one that is a lot easier to bear. Picture this: A world where everyone is required to carry a bag of sand. You have to walk around in life with a 50lb. bag of sand. You have to bring this sand everywhere you go at all times. Now imagine a kindhearted person sees you struggling and they come up and take your 50lb. bag and give you their 5lb. bag that has handles and is easier to carry. Isn't that a good trade off? You still have to carry the sand but not only is it less than you had originally, it's easier to handle.

Day 1

Is there a 50lb sandbag in your life? What is it? Are you ready to trade it out? Are you keeping it a secret? Do you ignore it? Why?

_____

Find three verses of scripture, three promises of God dealing with feeling tired, fed up and exhausted. As we go about this week, hide these scriptures in your heart.

_____

DAY 2

Dealing With People

Most of us know what it means to be sick and tired. And quite often, that mental and emotional exhaustion comes from having to deal with people. There have been many times in my life where I thought that I would be perfectly happy if people just didn't exist, if for just one day, they all disappeared. Maybe I'm the only one who've ever felt that way, though. However, one thing I am sure you can relate to is having a hard time loving some people. Certain people might get on your last nerve, but God tells us to love them just the same.

Read Matthew 5:38-48.

In this passage, Jesus tells His people (us) to love our enemies, to be good to those who use us, persecute us, take advantage of us and talk about us. These are the people you are to love and bless them and pray for them. When Jesus says to pray for them He doesn't mean to pray like David, that horrible and lasting torment come upon them. Jesus tells us to pray good things over them.

What makes you sick and tired?

_____

_____

_____

_____

_____

Day 2

When was the last time you blessed someone who hurt you?

___

How about prayed for someone who lied on you or gossiped about you? When did you last speak life over your enemy in prayer?

___

Think of one person (or more!) and write a quick prayer for them in the space below.

___

Dealing with people can be tough and sometimes the ones that irk you the most aren't those in the world, but your brothers and sisters in Christ. And yes, even Christians disagree sometimes. Yes, sometimes believers can be a bit too much to handle. And do you know who knew this well? Moses. We all know about Moses leading the Israelites out of Egypt and through the wilderness. But we have to remember that Moses never saw the promised land. Do you know why? Let's find out together.

Read Numbers 20:1-12.

The Israelites had been wondering in the desert of Zin for a while. Miriam, sister of Moses and Aaron, had just died and they'd run out of water. Just as we tend to do when we're inconvenienced, the people started complaining. They began speaking ill of Moses and Aaron and claiming they would rather die than go through. Looking back on it, the Israelites seem really dramatic, don't they? But we do the same thing. When our plans don't pan out the way we want or things seem to be taking a little too long, we start complaining.

WEEK FOUR

What are some things you tend to complain about?

_____
_____
_____
_____

What do you do about the things you listed above?

_____
_____
_____
_____
_____

Now both Moses and Aaron had been dealing with these complaints for a while and the people were getting on their last nerve. So, as they should have, they went to God for instruction.
Look at verse 8, what does the Lord tell Moses to do?

_____

Moses was told to speak to the rock but instead of being obedient to the Word of God, Moses does two things. What did Moses do?

_____

The people and their beasts were satisfied, they had their water and had finally stopped complaining. For now. But because Moses had disobeyed God, the Lord told him that he was not the one to bring the people into the promised land. To some, this may seem like a harsh punishment. Moses had come a long way, he'd been obedient and even though the people kept murmuring, complaining, doubting the authority and power of God. Moses had stayed true to his faith. So why did God have to be so harsh? Well, although Moses was a faithful servant, he allowed people (more importantly, the anger the people had stirred in him) to make him disobey the direct command of the Lord. His emotions were valid, but he shouldn't have allowed them to cause him to disobey.
Have you ever gotten so upset with someone that you did something you normally wouldn't?

Day 2

What happened?

_____

_____

How could you have acted differently?

_____

_____

_____

Moses got upset and the Bible says it's okay to get upset. However, the Word also gives us rules about handling our anger. Look up the two verses below and write down what they say about dealing with anger.

- Ephesians 4:26-27
- Ecclesiastes 7:9

The Lord knows that we may get angry from time to time but we should not be easily provoked nor should we allow our emotions to cause us to sin. In his case, Moses had had enough of the people of God. This was the straw that broke the camel's back, he got angry and disobeyed. Mind you, Moses wasn't angry with God, but he chose to be disobedient because he was angry with the people.

Is your anger easily provoked?

What is your first response to when you're furious? Do you "blow up" like Moses did?

_____

_____

What are some things that rile you up?

_____

_____

What calms you down?

_____

_____

Now look back at that situation in which you acted out of character. Would you have acted differently if given time to cool off?

_____

_____

Moses didn't have the chance to cool off and many times we won't either. But in these situations we cannot be like Moses. We have to act calmly and respond positively even if it is the last thing we want to do. Why? Because you can choose how you respond to a situation but you can't choose the consequences. I doubt that Moses would've struck the rock if he'd known that his actions would mean him dying in the wilderness and never seeing the promise of God fulfilled. What about you? Think this week about the consequences of your actions and, as Jesus tells us, pray for those who may have caused you to go too far.

DAY 3

When Exhaustion Turns Sour

Being fed up doesn't always lead to anger. Sometimes it leads to depression, a deep wallowing sadness that makes us feel alone. But as we learned in our earlier weeks, we are never alone because we have God on the inside of us. Elijah is one of the greatest prophets in the Bible. We all know him for his wonderful miracles and how God provided for him. He was a prayer warrior who always expected miracles from God. This man was so powerful in God that he didn't even die. When it was his time, God just pulled him up into Heaven. Don't believe me? Read 2 Kings 2:1-11. Elijah was a mighty man of God, but he was still a man and that means he had challenges that caused him to grow wear

Sometimes we get so caught up in the glamorous lives we imagine about the figures in the Bible had that we forget to see the person. With all the cool things Elijah did, it's easy to forget he was a normal human being. But he was. And there was a point in his ministry that Elijah was so tired, so drained, that He became both depressed and suicidal.

Read 1 Kings 18:25-19:7.

What do we learn about Elijah's character in chapter 18?

_____

_____

_____

How is this different from how he acts in chapter 19?

_____

_____

_____

Elijah goes from performing a great miracle and ridding the nation of all of Baal's prophets to running away, hiding and wishing he would die. That's a pretty major change, isn't it? You might think that Elijah was too sanctified to feel human emotions, and while he was chosen and imbued with power, he was just a man. As such, he felt sadness and that great, seemingly immeasurable sadness caused Elijah to give up.

Is it hard for you to believe that a person with an intimate relationship with God can be burdened with human weaknesses? Why?

_____

_____

_____

What are your weaknesses? Have they ever caused you to give up?

_____

_____

_____

Read over 1 Kings 19:4-7 again. Notice how Elijah actually prayed that the Lord would take his life. The Lord didn't and instead told the prophet to get up, eat and drink. Elijah was obedient but then he went and laid right back down. **That's what I want to point out.** Even as great as he was, Elijah could still feel sadness, it didn't just vanish into thin air. Elijah didn't simply get up and become cheerful, as though he'd never been depressed. Nope. In today's terminology, some might say that Elijah had high functioning depression. He could still do his duties and live what appeared to be a normal life, but on the inside his emotions were in turmoil. Sometimes it takes more than a kind word, we as people need to be lifted up so that we don't want to take the opportunity to lie back down.

Day 3

After such a magnificent victory for the kingdom of the Lord, we as readers, expect to see some sort of triumphant victory parade, not the man of God praying for death. And although Queen Jezebel was a formidable foe, we expect to see the prophet stand tall because of the God on his side. Guess what? Sometimes the unexpected happens. Things don't go according to plan and we feel sad when the world says we should rejoice. Elijah prayed for death right after a victory.

> *If you're feeling depressed, just know that it's okay to seek help, either from an elder in the church or a Christian counselor.*

Have you ever felt empty even after something good happened? Why do you think you felt this way?

___

___

___

Did you turn to God or even another person about it?

___

___

The prophet was told twice to get up and eat because being told once wasn't enough to bring him out of his sorrowful state. The angel of God had to touch him twice so don't feel like a failure if you need to be touched by the Lord. (Not even if it takes more than once.) We have to stay in a place of encouragement or else we'll allow exhaustion and stress to turn into depression. If you are feeling stressed, emotionally raw or sad, take some time to write out your feeling and ask God for a second touch.

Read 1 Kings 19:8-18.

What is Elijah feeling in verse 14? Why does he feel this way?

___

How does the Lord respond?

_____

_____

Elijah feels as though he is all alone, the sole upright person still fighting battles for the Lord. And while on mount Horeb he vents his frustrations to God. He is truly discouraged.

The prophet had a lot on his plate and those deep-seated frustrations turned into suicidal thoughts, they made him want to throw in the towel. But fellow believers, we cannot forget that Elijah went on to work for the Lord for many years after this emotional breakdown. God still had work for him to do and He carried him through the years, protecting him from Jezebel and those she sent to kill him. Elijah had reached a low point in chapter 18 but he didn't stay there. He came out of it and was still a crucial part of the Lord's work on the Earth.

You may not see it where you are right now but no matter how low you feel, it is not your destination, just a stop along the journey. The Father still has a plan for you and if you ask, He will give you a second touch and bring you from glory to glory. Don't give up, trouble won't last always.

> Psalm 30:1-5 King James Version (KJV)
> I will extol thee, O Lord; for thou hast lifted me up, and hast not made my foes to rejoice over me.
> O Lord my God, I cried unto thee, and thou hast healed me.
> O Lord, thou hast brought up my soul from the grave: thou hast kept me alive, that I should not go down to the pit.
> Sing unto the Lord, O ye saints of his, and give thanks at the remembrance of his holiness.
> For his anger endureth but a moment; in his favour is life: weeping may endure for a night, but joy cometh in the morning.

What does this passage mean to you?

_____

_____

_____

_____

_____

_____

_____

DAY 4

Loss And Self-Worth

It is natural to experience loss, whether it's financial or the loss of a loved one. To live in this world means to lose something eventually. But what do you do when you lose everything? How do you recover and recuperate?

What would you do in this situation? How do you think you would feel?

Naomi was a Jewish woman who moved to the nation of Moab with her husband Elimelech and her two sons and in only a few years, Naomi found herself in the position of being at a total loss.

Read Ruth 1:1-7.

For us, it may seem sad but not a complete loss for a woman to lose both her spouse and her sons but we must look at this passage in its cultural context, as we have done earlier in our study. Most women couldn't work, they weren't even considered citizens. That meant the only stable income they had came from their husbands, and when their husbands died, their sons. Furthermore, Naomi is currently living in Moab, a foreign country that worshipped many idols. Can you imagine living in a foreign country with no family and no one who shares your faith to talk to? That is the situation Naomi was in. She had her two daughter-in-laws but they were young and could easily marry again and live happy, stable lives. But Naomi was out of resources and her only option (other than prostitution or begging) was to return to Bethlehemjudah, her birthplace. Because of this she felt like the Lord Himself was against her.

WEEK FOUR

You are more than what you do or what you have.

Have you ever felt like you'd run out of options? What brought you to this place?

_____
_____
_____
_____
_____
_____
_____
_____
_____

Have you ever felt like God was out to get you?

_____
_____
_____
_____

Was your faith shaken?

_____
_____

Naomi had all but given up, she was ready to cut her losses. In verse 20 she even asks to be called "Mara" which means "bitter" while "Naomi" means "pleasant." According to verse 21, she felt

Day 4

empty. Luckily, Naomi had someone around her to encourage and support her: Ruth. Not only does Ruth agree to move to Judah and convert to Naomi's religion but she also promises to stay by her mother-in-law until death parts them and she goes to work gleaning in fields so that Naomi doesn't have to. To put it simply, Ruth had Naomi's back and supported her as best she could.

Is there a Ruth in your life? Someone who sticks by you in the tough times and helps you get back on your feet? If so, thank them this week. If not, ask God to bring you a Ruth.

Why do you think Ruth was so willing to go with Naomi?

_____

_____

Have you ever been a Ruth in someone else's situation?

_____

_____

_____

How did it end?

_____

_____

How did being a support system make you feel? Do you think it helped that person? Did it change you or your perspective in anyway?

_____

_____

_____

_____

Ruth could have left Naomi on her own, Naomi even encouraged her to do so because she felt no worth. In Naomi's eyes, she had nothing to offer her daughters, nothing to live for. She felt hopeless, insecure and unsure of her value. She tied her worth into her ability to have sons and provide a good home for her family and since she could no longer do either, she felt worthless. When you tie your worth into your actions you will always feel lacking. Naomi thought that she was only as good as what she was able to do, her accomplishments, her tasks. I used to feel the same way, that I was only as good as what I did and that if I didn't have this accomplishment or these letters after my name then I was worthless, a waste of space, useless.

Do you equate your actions to your worth?

___

When did you start? Why?

___

___

How does it make you feel?

___

___

In the world, what we accomplish can seem to be the only way we can give our lives meaning, to prove we matter. From early on, children are taught to seek out gold stickers and that those with gold stickers are better than those without. As an adult, this idea perpetuates itself in the media and if we allow it to, it becomes an integral part of our way of thinking. But you are not your accomplishments. Your identity does not equal your performance.

> *Before I formed thee in the belly I knew thee; and before thou camest forth out of the womb I sanctified thee, and I ordained thee a prophet unto the nations.*
>
> Jeremiah 1:5

> *For we are his workmanship, created in Christ Jesus unto good works, which God hath before ordained that we should walk in them.*
>
> Ephesians 2:10

> *I will praise thee; for I am fearfully and wonderfully made: marvellous are thy works; and that my soul knoweth right well.*
>
> Psalm 139:14

All three of these verses tell us that God made us. The God who made Heaven and Earth made us wonderfully in advance and knew us before we knew ourselves. What does this mean? We were who we are before we were even born! And God loved us way back then. Our worth isn't in what we do for a living or how much we make or how many social media followers we have.

Day 4

Our identity isn't in the feats we perform or the notoriety we achieve. Naomi was at the end of her rope, wanted to give up everything and wallow in her own bitterness because, in her eyes, she no longer had purpose. But if you finish the book of Ruth you find that Naomi becomes a wise counsellor to Ruth.

Dear friend, you have purpose, you have identity and even when you're going through the biggest loss of your life, remember Ruth and how she encouraged her mother-in-law. Remember the Holy Spirit who is our Counsellor and allow Him to encourage you.

It's okay to be tired. It's okay to feel lonely, but don't throw in the towel.

Use the space below to write some encouraging words for yourself and then take a few minutes to meditate on them.

_____
_____
_____
_____
_____

DAY 5

It's Not Just You

How many times have you thought that if you worked harder, if you did more, if people liked you more, that life wouldn't be so rough? We think to ourselves, if only I had this or could do that. Any of that sound familiar? The truth is, no matter who you are, if you're alive you will have troubles and tribulations. But as Christians we can thank God that we don't have to go through them alone.

> *These things I have spoken unto you, that in me ye might have peace. In the world ye shall have tribulation: but be of good cheer; I have overcome the world.*
>
> John 16:33

In this world, we'll go through tough times Nevertheless we'll go through because God is on our side.

No amount of money, no age, no success prevents you from dealing with trouble. Let's look at Paul who is a great example of this. Paul was a learned man, a religious scholar. He had a great lineage and was well-known.

Read Philippians 3:1-10.

Read 2 Corinthians 12:4-10.

Paul had a prestigious background and just looking at the table of contents in your Bible we can see that he wrote most of the New Testament but he still had troubles.

Day 5

What did Paul call his issue?

How many times did Paul ask God to take it away?

Sometimes we get so caught up in the exploits of the apostles that we pass over everything they had to go through. For instance, do you know that everywhere Paul went people tried to kill him? Literally, everywhere! He was whipped numerous times, imprisoned, beaten with rods and stoned plus a whole lot more. Feel free to read about it in 2 Corinthians 11:16-33. If accolades or degrees or any man-made standard could preclude you from suffering, don't you think Paul would've been a number one candidate? Here's something I want you to notice, while Paul had troubles, he never allowed them to hinder his walk with God or keep him from moving in his purpose. Yes, we get tired. Yes, we want to sit down and sleep for days and not have to deal with people but no matter how exhausted we feel we can't stop moving forward.

Write down some "if only" thoughts you've had.

Did "if only" happen? If so, did it help? If not, now that it's over do you think it would have?

What led you to believe that one day you wouldn't have trials anymore?

Is that Biblical?

In those times where you had "if only" thoughts, what helped you get through?

For even hereunto were ye called: because Christ also suffered for us, leaving us an example, that ye should follow his steps:

1 Peter 2:21

We suffer because Christ suffered and we are no better than Him but in our suffering God is an ever-present help (Psalm 46:1). Even in the midst of troubling and tiring issues we can have hope. Find the verses below and write down the encouragement offered in each.

- Romans 8:28
- Isaiah 41:10
- 1 John 5:4
- John 14:27
- Psalm 34:6

Our Father is good and He never leaves us alone or unprepared. Even though trouble is always around remember that you are an overcomer.

DAY 6

Desperation

*L*et's dive right into the Word! Read Genesis 25:21-34.

I don't want to discuss whether or not Jacob's actions were honorable (we all know how Jacob treats Esau later), I want to focus on Esau.

Read verse 29 again. What does the Bible say about Esau?

Esau was faint, in fact the Bible states he was on the brink of death but his own little brother wouldn't give him a bit of soup. Not until Esau gave up his right to the majority of the land, his right to lead the family and a whole lot more. But Esau was hungry and he was desperate and so he gave away something he could never get back.

Have you ever felt desperate? What was the situation?

_____

Were you willing to do anything to ease the burden?

_____

Did that desperation get you into trouble?

_____

According to the world, desperate times call for desperate measures but according to God desperate times call for prayer and fasting, they call for more time spent in the Word of God. Esau felt like he was at death's door, he was willing to risk it all and from that point on he had a steady losing streak. As believers, we don't have to give into our feelings of desperation or weariness. Nor do we have to give up.

> *And I heard a great voice out of heaven saying, Behold, the tabernacle of God is with men, and he will dwell with them, and they shall be his people, and God himself shall be with them, and be their God.*
> *And God shall wipe away all tears from their eyes; and there shall be no more death, neither sorrow, nor crying, neither shall there be any more pain: for the former things are passed away.*
>
> Revelation 21:3-4

Our God is the wiper of tears, He is the lifter or heads. He heals the brokenhearted and fixes their wounds (Psalm 141:3). Sometimes, even for those mature in the faith, it can be a tough battle not to give up when the situation looks bleak but when we give up we find ourselves in a domino effect, much like Esau. In the passage we read, Esau sold his birthright, later in the story he is tricked out of a blessing. Esau, although he was the firstborn son, is left with basically nothing and it all started when he gave into desperation. Desperation can make us feel hopeless and at times it seems like there is no end in sight.

Esau felt desperate and gave up everything for short-term satisfaction that faded soon after. Desperation can cause you to give up on what God has for you and let's be real, that is exactly what the enemy wants. Satan wants you to feel so desperate that you lose sight of the bigger picture, just as Esau lost sight of all he was losing. When you give into desperation, you're giving up a lot more than you think.

Have you ever given into desperation and then realized that your choice led you to somewhere you didn't want to be? What happened?

_____

_____

_____

Looking back now, would you have made the same decision?

_____

_____

_____

We may feel lost, lonely, unsure or even at our wit's end but instead of giving in, we have to give it up to God.

But, desperation isn't always a bad thing. Read Mark 5:25-34.

Day 6

The woman with the issue of blood had been going through her trial for 12 long years. She was seen as unclean, an outcast and had spent all she had on doctors that couldn't help her. She was desperate enough to try one more time. She'd heard of Jesus and her desperation caused her to break the law by going into a crowded place and do something most would consider insane: touch the hem of His garment. In this case, desperation led to healing and restoration. In response to desperate situations, don't be like Esau and seek temporary satisfaction, be like the woman in this passage of Scripture. When you are desperate, run to Jesus, run to the Healer, the Restorer, the Giver and the Gift and you'll have all you need.

Are you feeling desperate? In the space below, talk to God. Write down how you feel and what you're expecting him to do. And if you aren't feeling this way, take time to thank God for all the situations He has brought you through.

_____

_____

_____

_____

_____

_____

_____

_____

I want you to write your own Nevertheless statements. Fill in the declarations below.

I am having issues Nevertheless _____

I am in a desperate situation Nevertheless _____

I feel weary Nevertheless _____

_____ Nevertheless _____

Repeat these statements to yourself each day for the next week.

My prayer for you is that you never allow your situation to hinder your walk, that no matter how desperate times appear that you turn to God instead of looking for answers in someone or something else. I pray these things for you in the name of Jesus Christ, our King. Amen.

DAY 7

You Can Keep Going

We've made it to the end of our study and I just want to thank you all for taking this journey with me and say that I am proud of you. In order to benefit from this study, you had to be vulnerable, you may have had to rip off a few bandages or open the skeleton closet of your mind. That takes courage and determination and you did it.

To finish off our week on feeling fed up or ready to throw in the towel, I want to focus on ways to keep going. The Word of God says we will get weary, life is full of trouble and that won't change. But thanks be to God that we have the strength to endure even the toughest battles. Look up the verses below and write a sentence or two about how you personally can apply it to your life and maybe even to your current situation. Be specific, write this like a plan of action so that you can grow into who God has called you to be.

- Matthew 11:28-30
- Psalm 55:22
- 1 Peter 4:19
- Isaiah 40:31
- Philippians 4:8-9

Throughout the course of this study it has been my goal to give you pointers on how to apply the concepts in this book, not just give you a list. Think of the exercise you just completed as a game plan against weariness. You did it! You just took the first step toward having the victory when weariness comes against you. Never forget what Jesus says in John 14:26-27:

WEEK FOUR

But the Comforter, which is the Holy Ghost, whom the Father will send in my name, he shall teach you all things, and bring all things to your remembrance, whatsoever I have said unto you.

Peace I leave with you, my peace I give unto you: not as the world giveth, give I unto you. Let not your heart be troubled, neither let it be afraid.

The New American Standard Bible (NASB) calls the Holy Spirit a Helper. That means when we are going through some difficult battles and we're doing our best, the Holy Spirit is there to help get us through, to rejuvenate us and remind us of the promises of God. That being said, I want to remind you of the truths we learned in our time together. Below each affirmation write how it makes you feel, how you can apply it, how it relates to you. Think of this last day together as a way to write your vision and make it plain because only then can you actually put it into action (Habakkuk 2:2).

- Even when I feel worthless, God paid it all for me.
- I may struggle with loneliness Nevertheless God is always walking alongside me.
- Sometimes I worry Nevertheless I can cast all my cares on Him.
- The world may make me weary Nevertheless with God I can soar on eagle's wings.

_____
_____
_____
_____
_____
_____
_____
_____

Never forget that it's okay to go to someone else when you need help. Don't be ashamed of the struggles you are dealing with. There's no shame nor condemnation for those in Christ Jesus (Romans 8:1)!

I hope this study has blessed you. I pray that you remember what you've learned and that you apply it to your life and that with each battle you grow stronger in the Lord. You may feel weak nevertheless in the Lord you are strong.

Nevertheless Affirmations

*I feel down Nevertheless,
I am encouraged*

*I'm not perfect Nevertheless,
I am chosen*

*I don't know what to do
Nevertheless God is
my champion*

*I'm tired Nevertheless
I can keep going.*

About the Author

Chyina Powell is an editor and writer at Powell Editorial. She is the financial chair of the Alumni Epsilon chapter of the International English Honors' Society, Sigma Tau Delta and her writing interests lie mainly in speculative fiction and creative nonfiction. With years of editorial and publishing experience as well as a Master's in Creative Writing from the University of Pennsylvania, Chyina is passionate about her work and shining a light on those voices previously unheard or misrepresented.

Connect with her on Instagram or on her website!

https://www.powelleditorial.org

www.ingramcontent.com/pod-product-compliance
Lightning Source LLC
Chambersburg PA
CBHW051119110526
44589CB00026B/2983